LIFE AFTER DEATH

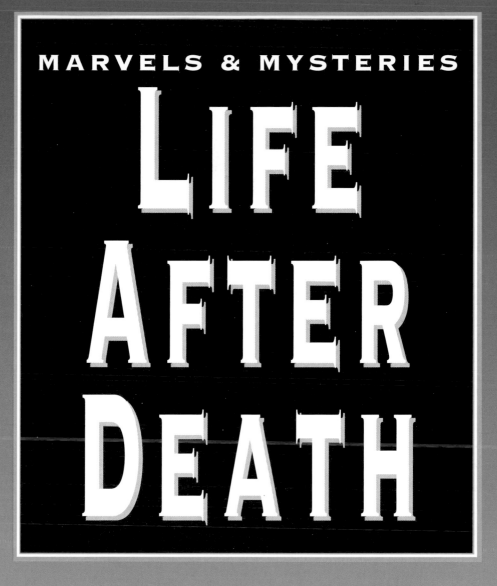

MARVELS & MYSTERIES

LIFE AFTER DEATH

This material has previously appeared in
partwork form as *The Unexplained*

Published in 1997 by Parragon
Unit 13-17 Avonbridge Trading Estate,
Atlantic Road, Avonmouth, Bristol BS11 9QD
All rights reserved

ISBN 0-7525-1212-9

Printed and bound in Italy

CONTENTS

INTRODUCTION

People are probably the only creatures on earth who know that one day they will die. The nature of death, and what happens next, have been major concerns of mankind since the dawn of man's history, and are a cornerstone of most of the world's religions. Stone Age people created elaborate tombs and buried their peers with personal possessions to help them in a physical afterlife, while the civilization of ancient Egyptians was created on the premise that death was not an end, but a departure into new realms.

This book looks at ancient and modern ideas about survival after death, and examines the evidence for and against them. Inevitably, much of the evidence is arguable. Most of it comes from seance rooms and professional mediums, those who claim to be able to contact and converse with the spirits of the dead. Enormously popular in the late 19th and early 20th centuries, Spiritualism at one time seemed set to become an established religion in its own right, but accusations of fraud by sceptics, photographic evidence of trickery and the confessions of some mediums have driven it underground once again. Some mediums, though, have never been 'caught out' in this way.

Spiritualism is not the whole story. There is, too, the testimony of those who have 'died' for short periods, then been brought back to life by medical science. Other people remember past lives, sometimes spontaneously, but usually under hypnosis. Past lives may be remembered in detail, but are difficult to check. If the previous life was famous and well-recorded, then the person remembering it may be parroting something they have read, while if it was obscure, there is very little to check it against. You, the reader, will have to assess the evidence and draw your own conclusions about whether there really is life after death.

**THE ONE GREAT CERTAINTY FOR EVERYONE IS
DEATH. YET HOW MANY OF US BOTHER TO
CONSIDER – LET ALONE PREPARE FOR – THIS
HIGHLY SIGNIFICANT PART OF LIFE?**

What happens when we die? Nothing? Complete bliss – 'eternal life'? Or a vague, insubstantial something? Materialists and atheists would, of course, answer 'nothing'. For them, life is a purely biological process; when the body dies, the personality dies with it, just as electricity stops being generated when a battery fails. To such people, life cannot 'go somewhere else'.

These rationalists frequently point out that the age-old belief in an afterlife is merely a reflection of Man's terror of death and personal oblivion. Throughout history, he has either avoided the unthinkable or surrounded it with ritual and a childish optimism. Materialists believe this to be craven and intellectually dishonest: we ought to face 'the

In his painting **The Plains of Heaven**, *below,* **the English painter John Martin presents a vision of the afterlife in which hosts of the blessed rejoice in a dramatic landscape worthy of the mid-Victorian Romantic poets. These angels, some of them winged, play the traditional harp.**

facts', they say – after all, it has to be admitted that the one sure fact of life for everyone is death.

So what of the concept of 'eternal life'? Nearly all religionists have preached that we survive bodily death in one form or another. It is probably also true to say that the more sophisticated the religion, the more certainly it envisages some form of life everlasting, whether in a kind of paradise or amid the torments of hell.

If the materialists are correct, no further enquiry need be made. But if the religionists are right, then it surely behoves each individual to look to his or her salvation. But any belief in an afterlife must remain a matter of faith, and only the experience of our own death can prove us either right or wrong.

But what if neither of these rigid concepts is correct? What if 'something' – some lifespark or vestige of the human personality – survives and enters a new kind of existence, not as a form of reward or punishment, but merely as part of some natural law? Today, many psychical researchers feel that the balance of evidence suggests that 'something' does survive, not necessarily for very long after

WHAT HAPPENS AFTER DEATH?

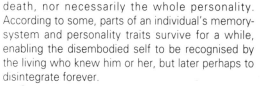

death, nor necessarily the whole personality. According to some, parts of an individual's memory-system and personality traits survive for a while, enabling the disembodied self to be recognised by the living who knew him or her, but later perhaps to disintegrate forever.

Objective analysis of purported evidence for human survival is a major concern of the Society for Psychical Research (SPR), founded in London in 1882. But the founding of the SPR would probably never have happened but for events of a generation earlier, which themselves might never have occurred but for the emancipation of Man's thought that began in the Renaissance.

As the horizons of knowledge expanded, the materialist position strengthened; and by the mid 19th century, a 'thinker' was generally reckoned to be someone who had freed himself from the trammels of 'superstition'. Religionists, feeling themselves under attack, tended to close their minds to any facts that undermined their position, ironically adopting much the same attitude that some scientists take even today when confronted with overwhelming evidence for certain paranormal events.

In the light of such hard rationalism, a faith with results that could be demonstrated was highly sought after. So when poltergeist activity occurred at the Fox family home in Hydesville, New York, in

The building, far left, is a reconstruction of the Fox family's historic home in Hydesville, New York, where the modern Spiritualist movement was born.

The strange rappings and table-turnings that occurred in the presence of the Fox sisters, left, were taken by many to be the long-awaited proof of communications from the dead.

1848, the public was tremendously excited. Here, at last, was 'proof' of the survival of the spirit; an antidote to the bleakness of materialism. Spiritualism was born and has since become a significant movement in the western world.

Spiritualists believe that their faith demonstrates incontrovertibly the existence of life after death. They point to seances where, it is said, spirits move heavy tables, play musical instruments and introduce apports; where dead relatives and friends speak recognisably in their own voices of events known only to themselves and one or more of the sitters, and sometimes even materialise in their own appearances before them.

But scientists of the time refused to investigate seance-room phenomena, while Spiritualists – and fundamentalist Christians – took refuge (though not as allies) in a simple faith that regarded any such discoveries as due to Devil-inspired cleverness.

OBJECTIVE ASSESSMENT

It was in this climate of extremes that the SPR was founded. Initial members included a group of British intellectuals who objected to the entrenched positions of 'believers' and 'sceptics' and who felt that objective assessment of unusual phenomena was long overdue. Since then, the material collected by the British SPR and similar societies in other countries provides the strongest clues for the serious enquirer into the nagging question: 'What happens when we die?'

The huge body of material collected since 1882 may be categorised as follows: phantasms; communications through mediums; cross-correspondences; 'drop-in' communicators; 'welcoming' phantasms, seen by the dying; experiences of patients during 'clinical death'; out-of-the-body experiences; cipher and combination-lock tests; appearance pacts; evidence for reincarnation; and electronic voice phenomena.

▮▮ WE ENCOUNTER THE DEAD AT THE

MOMENT OF GOING TO SLEEP, AND

AGAIN AT THE MOMENT OF WAKING ...

THESE MOMENTS OF WAKING AND

GOING TO SLEEP ARE OF THE UTMOST

SIGNIFICANCE FOR INTERCOURSE

WITH THE SO-CALLED DEAD AND WITH

OTHER SPIRITUAL BEINGS OF THE

HIGHER WORLDS. **▮▮**

DR RUDOLF STEINER,

THE DEAD ARE WITH US

In **The Treasures of Satan** *by the* **late 19th-century French symbolist Jean Delville**, left, *Satan is depicted flame-coloured as a sign of both his lust and his fiery destruction of souls through degradations of the flesh.*

Burial of the dead is not universal. In the artist's impression, below **left,** *a Red Indian brave visits the rotting corpses of members of his tribe, exposed to the elements and birds of prey on a hill set apart for this purpose. Their spirits were believed to spend eternity in the so-called Happy Hunting Ground.*

The SPR's first great achievement was a census of hallucinations. Seventeen thousand replies to a questionnaire about the prevalence of hallucinatory experiences were collected, and of these – after all possible explanations were exhausted – about 8 per cent remained as apparently genuine experiences. These were critically examined by the leading members of the SPR and upon the findings were based two volumes, *Apparitions of the Living* and *Human Personality and its Survival of Physical Death*. Listed in the former were several apparitions of people said to have appeared up to 12 hours after their deaths. Researchers felt that these might be due to thought transference from the newly dead individual to his living contacts, delayed perhaps until conditions were right for it to appear. Even so, a number of these cases can still be classified as evidence of – at least temporary – survival.

Most parapsychologists accepting evidence of phantasms agree that thought transference – which includes thoughts, feelings, and images both visual and auditory, and which would today be classified under the heading of extra-sensory perception (ESP) – is a faculty of some human minds and could be used to explain phantasms of the living. This also seems to be confirmed by the claims of certain individuals who say that they can 'think' themselves into paying 'astral visits' – travelling while out-of-the-body – to acquaintances. Claimants not only 'see' the rooms into which they project themselves mentally but report accurately such features as changes of furniture, of which their conscious selves were ignorant. Furthermore, they are often seen by the friends they 'visit', and are sometimes also accurately described by strangers who happen to be present.

However, some 6 or 7 per cent of the apparitions recorded in the SPR survey appeared too long after death for them to be explained as delayed telepathic communications. This small number of cases remained after all other explanations – hoaxing, exaggeration, mistaken identity, dreaming and so on – had been examined and found inadequate.

Intriguingly, those cases classified as genuine apparitions or phantasms of the dead showed certain common features. In some, the apparition conveyed information previously unknown to the percipient. In others, it seemed to have a clearly

▮▮ ACCORDING TO VARIOUS COMMUNICATORS, THERE ARE OTHER PLANES THAT ARE INCONCEIVABLE TO US... BUT UNLESS THE EVIDENCE OF PHYSICAL RESEARCH IS AN ENORMOUS CONFIDENCE TRICK... THE INDIVIDUAL SURVIVES DEATH IN A FORM NOT UNLIKE HIS PRESENT MODE OF BEING. ▮▮

COLIN WILSON, AFTERLIFE

A 'mental' sensitive may go into a trance, in which a 'control' (otherwise known as a 'controlling spirit' or 'spirit guide') speaks through him or her, frequently in an entirely different voice, occasionally even giving her a different appearance, so that a European woman may temporarily take on the likeness and voice of, say, a Chinese man.

Through the sensitive, the control may also introduce other alleged spirits, recognisable by voice, gesture, or the nature of the private information given to one of the sitters at the seance. Such so-called spirits may seem extremely convincing, though it must be admitted that those who want to believe will probably believe anyway. However, sensitives often have striking gifts of clairaudience, clairvoyance and other forms of ESP. Sometimes, they will communicate through the planchette board, through automatic script, or through drawings in the style of recognised masters, or compositions in the manner of famous musicians.

Another type of sensitive is the 'direct voice' medium, who does not, as a rule, go into a trance but from whose vicinity voices of both sexes and different kinds speak in various accents, and sometimes even other, identifiable languages.

Communications from such sources vary enormously in quality, but much of it is trivial and curiously materialistic. It was even a frequent gibe in the early days of Spiritualism that spirits seemed to spend their afterlife smoking cigars and drinking whisky. Yet such 'materialistic' evidence would support the teaching of some Eastern religions that an early stage after death involves passing through

defined purpose. In yet others, it resembled a dead person unknown to the percipient who later recognised him from a portrait or photograph, or from some characteristic of the deceased unknown to him at the time. Sometimes, too, different people at different times – independently of each other – saw the same apparition.

CONTINUING DESIRES

Some psychical researchers think that only those cases in which apparitions indicate a specific purpose for their manifestation can be taken as significant evidence of survival and even then perhaps only as evidence of temporary survival. It could well be that, as a memory survives the event remembered, so a desire to communicate something urgently to the living might continue to exist after the thinker's death until its purpose is fulfilled: then it, too, might die.

Since the early days of the Society for Psychical Research, many astute minds have studied and recorded evidence of supposed survival provided by such apparitions. Some have believed that we live on, others not. But it is safe to say that none of the researchers involved has ever become convinced of survival on the evidence of apparitions alone.

While phantasms were being investigated by the SPR, so, too, were the activities of mediums – or, as they are better named, sensitives. These are people (more often women than men) who have unusual psychic talents, which they display in various ways. According to their specific gifts, they are generally classified as either 'mental' or 'physical' sensitives.

A representation of a Viking galley is shown, above, being burned at the climax of the annual Up Helly festival at Lerwick in the Shetland Isles. Ancient Viking funerals combined cremation with dramatic spectacle, the dead being placed in a burial ship which was set alight as it was pushed out to sea. It must have seemed to mourners on the shore that the journey to Valhalla (the Viking heaven) was a very real and even physical one.

Peruvian Incas, right, are seen burying a chief and preparing him for an afterlife just as stylish and prosperous as his earthly existence. Like many other pagan peoples, they buried treasure, food and weapons with their dead, believing these artefacts to be necessary if they were to survive in the next world in the manner to which they were accustomed. Others, however – such as the Balinese, seen in front of a pagoda-like cremation tower far right, top – do not hold possessions important for the life to come.

Very popular at Edwardian seances was the moulding of 'spirit' hands in paraffin wax. The hands were believed to dematerialise, leaving the moulds unbroken. But Harry Houdini, the great escape artist and scourge of fraudulent mediums, top left, proved that it was a relatively easy trick to learn.

a realm of illusion where the ego may indulge in anything and everything it wants.

Other communications, however, are of a highly ethical and literary standard. Yet, frequently, when challenged to give an unequivocal description of what awaits us on the other side of life, communicators reply (perhaps not unreasonably) that the spirit existence is indescribable. Some rare spirits are more forthcoming, though; and an uncannily consistent picture of the afterlife emerges through their communications.

'Physical' mediums are those in whose presence, whether they go into trances or not, physical phenomena occur, such as loud raps from the seance table or from various points around the room, perhaps. Sometimes these seem to be in an intelligent code, as if trying to convey some message. Also common are telekinetic phenomena (solid objects moving as if handled by an invisible person); levitation – of the sensitive or of objects; the playing of musical instruments by unseen hands; and actual materialisation of spirit forms.

Sadly, in the short history of Spiritualism, many of these phenomena have been faked, but there still remain many cases of genuine physical mediumship that defy 'rational' explanation. Many tests have been set up to try to trap the frauds, and, to a lesser extent, to determine the extent of the phenomena. One such test involved the provision of a dish of warm wax at a physical seance. The materialised 'spirit' hand dipped itself into the wax, which rapidly set. The hand then dematerialised, leaving the mould unbroken. Astonished witnesses took this as a certain sign of life after death.

FACES FROM THE PAST

MEDIUMS WHO TAKE ON THE FACIAL FEATURES OF THE DECEASED ARE RARE INDEED; BUT QUEENIE NIXON, WHEN ENTRANCED, ACTUALLY UNDERWENT SUCH TRANSFIGURATIONS

In the half-light, people gasped as the woman before them acquired the features and spoke with the voices of loved ones who were long dead. This was not a scene of terror from a Hollywood movie, and the reactions of the audience were those of joy and hope – for this was Queenie Nixon, one of the rare transfiguration mediums, at work. The public demonstrations that she gave over many years, from the 1950s onwards, may have appeared outwardly sensational, but underneath lay a story of devotion, purpose and selfless hard work.

Queenie Nixon was an only child whose father died 11 weeks before she was born. She was brought up in the English town of Kettering, Northamptonshire, by two aunts who were dedicated Spiritualists and mediums. Consequently, she virtually lived at the local Spiritualist Church. 'I've never known anything else,' she said. 'I always have been and always will be a Spiritualist.'

She joined the Spiritualist Sunday school, where the teaching made a lasting impression on her. By the age of eight, Queenie was also sitting in on seances – 'just to be there'. This helped earn her the nickname of 'Spooks' at school. It was at the age of 14, while in the advanced group at the Sunday school, that her psychic ability began to develop. Queenie already knew how much personal sacrifice and discipline would be required of her should she use her gifts as a medium, and she felt eager and willing to give what she could.

In describing how she became aware of her developing powers, she said: 'I used to feel myself drifting away, and I could hear myself talking, saying things I hadn't even been thinking, and using philosophical expressions beyond my normal vocabulary.' This phenomenon continued, and her own voice gradually became fainter whenever she 'drifted away', until sometimes she could not even hear what she herself was saying. Then: 'One day I heard a change of intonation, and thought, "It can't be me. That's not my voice!" By now, the spirit forces had perfected the procedure of withdrawing and returning me to my body.'

During this period, she became aware of her spirit guides. One was Paul, a young aristocrat from the reign of George III, who had died at the age of 29. The other was Sister Edith, a missionary from Dover in Kent, who also died young, at only 28.

It was Paul who suggested that Queenie might have potential as a physical medium. But, at 19, although she was already leading services within the Spiritualist Church and steadily developing, she did not feel ready to undertake mediumistic work. In fact, Queenie Nixon did not form her first circle until she was 23, by which time she was married and living in Blackpool. Within three weeks of the first sitting, discarnate voices began to take part in the seances. This phenomenon then ceased as suddenly as it had started, and nothing further happened for some time.

SEANCE CIRCLE

The young medium spent the next few years bringing up her two children and helping her husband with the arduous work of running their horticultural nurseries just outside Chesterfield in Derbyshire. But she still found the time to work in the Spiritualist churches in the area. In about 1950, she felt she had put down roots at last, and formed a new seance circle. The results were startling.

Sitters began to observe something like cigarette smoke swirling round Queenie's head. Next, there appeared white outlines of faces, like silhouettes, distinct but not solid. At one sitting, several members independently observed eyes in these faces, which next came to resemble theatrical masks, becoming ever more detailed and clear.

According to Queenie Nixon, the moment had arrived when the spirit guides had completed their experiments and had perfected a way to communicate through her. This method was transfiguration, or 'moulding', in which the medium's face and voice become like those of the dead communicator.

After the 1950s, Queenie Nixon's seances became even more remarkable. But the medium

herself was able to say little about them because she would go into such a deep trance that she could not recall anything that may have happened. After preparing for her work through intense prayer and concentration, she would relax when the seance started, thinking: 'Here I am. Take me away'. And that would be the last she knew until she awoke. When she 'returned', there would be a fog before her eyes and her vision was temporarily blurred. She was able to recollect what transpired only if there had been some disturbance, in which case she would often feel very ill. 'It isn't easy for me to answer questions accurately,' she confided. 'I don't work consciously.'

Two Yorkshire residents, Pat Walkington of Huntington and Mary Staddon of York, have given a description of the Queenie Nixon transfiguration seance they attended in Harrogate in 1981. They entered a well-lit room and sat right at the front, in order to have a clear view. The medium came into the room and was helped to put up a screen made of a black sheet suspended over a wire. (This, Queenie explained, was not to create an air of mystery, but to reduce the possibility of illusion from the background.) Then, Pat Walkington recounts:

'They put a table on the rostrum in front of the screen, on which Mrs Nixon placed a small lamp with a red bulb which tilted up to illuminate her face. She put on a black blouse to cover her clothes and sat down a few feet above us on the platform. We were so close, we could see nothing was rigged. The lights were extinguished and her light switched on simultaneously. It was not pitch dark and, when my eyes had adjusted to the dim glow given by her lamp, I could see the clock well enough to tell the time.'

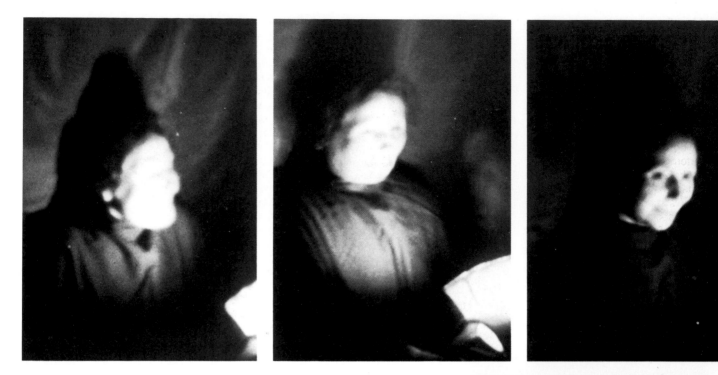

The voice of the spirit-guide, Paul, then gave an invocation and told the audience what would happen. It was explained that he did this because he felt the public were owed an explanation about transfiguration, and he tried to make it as scientific as possible. To many, Paul's words were one of the most fascinating parts of the seance.

SPIRIT GUIDES

On this occasion, a female spirit healer also spoke briefly after Paul. Then the medium's head dropped forward – and when she lifted it, she was transformed into the spirit guide, Sister Edith. 'It was as if another person had changed places with her; but that was impossible!' Pat Walkington exclaimed. It was the spirit guide, Sister Edith – who also appeared between each set of transfigurations – who now took control of the proceedings. Using five or six pieces of information that were given by the communicator and also by a process of elimination, she found the correct recipient for the mouldings. Sister Edith then asked: 'Are you ready to receive your mouldings?' At the answer 'Yes', the medium's head dropped again.

'When she lifted her head,' said Pat Walkington, 'you could see a white cloud and a triangular shape – nose, mouth and corners of eyes. Then, as you watched, you saw it moulded into a face.'

The transfiguration would take about eight seconds, and the audience was encouraged to talk at this point, but as the witness declared: 'At the same time, you daren't take your eyes off her as it is so interesting.' There were about 20 mouldings on that evening in 1981, though it is said that double that number were often received.

Some recipients were too dumbfounded to react at first; but because response and recognition helped to strengthen and clarify the mouldings, the recipients were invited to talk to their communicator. The communicators usually said very little, but seemed to get much across through facial expressions and nods.

The three obviously very different transfiguration mouldings, above, were recorded on camera during seances. Of the mouldings she produced, Queenie Nixon commented: 'None of them resembles me and it is just not possible for me to manipulate my own face to produce such a variety of size and shape and profile'.

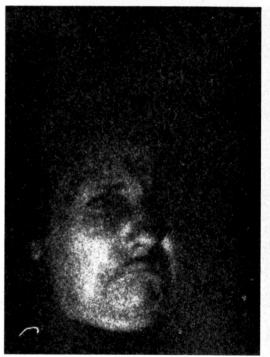

Taken by a professional photographer using a fast film, the moulding of a masculine face with a moustache, right, was recognised by the photographer as one of his own dead relatives.

> TO QUEENIE NIXON, ALL THAT MATTERED WAS TO GIVE PEOPLE THE CONVICTION OF THE FAITH THEY ARE SUPPOSED TO HAVE – THAT THIS PHYSICAL LIFE ISN'T THE BEGINNING AND END OF EVERYTHING.

Mary Staddon received the first contact of the evening with evidence that pointed unmistakably to her. She was given her father's name, religious background and birth date. She was also given her own birthday, the date of her mother's death and some details of her current personal circumstances. Then Sister Edith asked if she was ready to receive her moulding. Mary Staddon 'hoped beyond hope' for her mother, who had died in 1969. But when the moulding began, a long, slim face with aquiline features formed. Her disappointment turned to excitement, however, as a pronounced widow's peak, a moustache and piercing eyes confirmed the presence of someone equally close to her. Later she laughed about it, saying: 'It wasn't so much my father I was after, but trust him to get first in the queue!' The witness was reduced to tears but, mindful that she should keep talking to maintain the communication, she composed herself quickly. Mary Staddon had a strong voice, and was convinced that this helped to achieve the clarity and long duration of her father's moulding.

When her father gave her one of the long, slow winks she remembers from childhood, laughter spread through the hall. 'He told me to keep my

The photograph, below left, was taken just at the moment when one moulding was melting away and another building up. Queenie Nixon said of this: 'The mask which is disappearing to the left has obviously been a smaller and younger person.'

Of the moulding below, Queenie Nixon said: 'This shows a long straight nose, but my nose was broken as a child and has a bump on the bridge and a slight tilt at the base.'

weren't prepared for the shock... She looked tired, ill and green... and it took about 20 minutes for her to get back to normal.'

Once, a hypnotist was asked, in her presence, if he could hypnotise the entire audience into thinking they were seeing what they were expected to see. 'Certainly, I could,' he replied, 'but I could not hypnotise a camera.' He said this in the light of some remarkable photographic evidence for Queenie Nixon's transfigurations. One set of pictures was taken at Batley Carr, West Yorkshire, in September 1967 by D.M. Hosley – at that time, a technician in the psychology department of the University of Leeds. He did so out of scientific interest. Another set, by a professional photographer from Bristol of his own communicators – his father, uncle and mother – was taken in the 1970s.

Queenie Nixon willingly co-operated with psychical researchers; and, in 1982, she accepted an invitation to be investigated at Harvard University in the United States, submitting herself to such studies even though she knew that she might be laying herself open to criticism and controversy. She found it ironic that, although 'it is not wrong to have faith' in life after death, 'it is wrong to prove it'.

  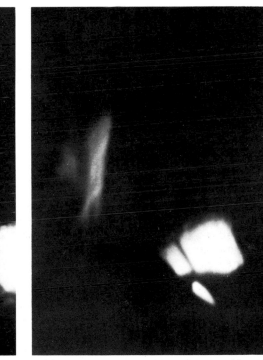

pecker up – one of his old expressions.' As he faded, another face took form – 'the whole jowls and puffy round face of my Nan. She was a real Grandma. I saw her face, her earrings and her distinctive smile.'

Mary Staddon received yet a third moulding – that of an aunt with whom she had lived. Although the last two mouldings were more fleeting, less well defined and with less strength of voice, they were immediately recognisable to the witness. Having lost these three important people in her life in the space of less than a month, she felt specially happy and grateful for this reunion.

Pat Walkington finished the account: 'We'd been warned not to be surprised by Mrs Nixon's appearance at the end of the seance. But we

The photograph, above right, is remarkable in that Queenie did not appear on the negative when the film was developed, even though she was sitting in her usual place in relation to the lamp at the time the picture was taken. The photograph is one of a series taken during a group seance, and is inexplicable to those who were present.

In spite of Queenie Nixon's wish to convince people of survival after death, she declined offers of television appearances because, she said, publicity might give a distorted view of her work, and the results of her seances were of more importance to her than fame. Requests for her help multiplied, and she attempted to answer as many as she could, travelling widely with her husband, Clifford.

Her workload was at times very arduous; but to Queenie Nixon, all that mattered was 'to give people the conviction of the faith they are supposed to have – that this physical life isn't the beginning and end of everything.

To the many thousands who were given joy and a sense of new direction in their lives, that was all that mattered, too.

IS DEATH A DREAM?

IF, AS MATERIALIST PHILOSOPHERS BELIEVE, THE MIND IS MERELY A SHADOW OF THE BRAIN, THERE IS NO POSSIBILITY THAT CONSCIOUSNESS SURVIVES DEATH. BUT MANKIND STILL HAS A TENACIOUS BELIEF IN THE AFTERLIFE. IS THIS FAITH REALLY JUSTIFIED?

The overwhelming majority of Mankind has always taken it for granted that some aspect of the human personality survives bodily death. In many societies, ancestors are considered to live on in a rather shadowy form in a netherworld, where they can be contacted by shamans through dreams or trances. In the East, hundreds of millions of people are convinced that the core of the personality survives bodily death and comes back to this world in another physical body via the process of rebirth or reincarnation. And Muslims and Christians have generally believed in various kinds of afterlife that seem to depend for their nature on a person's faith and actions during his or her life.

By contrast, those who are followers of the philosophy of materialism fervently deny that any aspect of personal consciousness can survive the death of the physical body. They believe that the mind is nothing but an aspect, or a kind of shadow, of the activity of the brain. All mental activity must therefore cease completely when the brain stops functioning at the time of death. However, in spite of the fact that many highly educated people believe it, this theory of materialism has no truly persuasive logical or scientific basis.

A grotto of ancestor figures, below, overlooks growing crops at Toraja, inset, on the island of Sulawesi (formerly Celebes) in Indonesia. The inhabitants of the island believe that, in some sense, the spirits of their ancestors live on in the effigies, and that they can ensure a good harvest.

But if, in contrast to the beliefs of the materialists, there *is* some sort of personal survival of bodily death, what is it like? The usual answer is to say it is a life of the soul. But what precisely is the soul? Is it, perhaps, what we normally think of as the mind? And if so, what kind of existence can the mind have without the physical body? We are so used to living in a physical form that it is almost impossible to imagine ourselves surviving without some kind of body. Certainly, our physical bodies disintegrate after our death.

One answer to these questions is suggested by the experience of dreaming. In dreams, we find ourselves in all sorts of places and situations. We see and hear things, talk to people and also move about. But meanwhile, the physical body is lying asleep in bed. So the body in which we find our-

selves in dreams cannot be our own body: it must be another body, which can conveniently be referred to as the 'dream body'. This dream body, like our physical body in waking life, is usually taken for granted within the dream and so seems real enough. Normally, it is only on waking up that we realise that we were dreaming, and that the dream world and dream body we experienced were not in fact what we would accept as being physically real.

In order to wake up, we need the living physical body. After death, of course, this is no longer possible. But perhaps we continue to exist in a kind of dream state from which we cannot awake. In this state, the dream body will seem real, and so will the world we experience, but it will not be physical – any more than our ordinary dreams are physical.

Fascinating insights into the nature of the dream world arise in lucid dreams, within which the dreamer becomes aware that he is dreaming. These are relatively rare, but many people have had occasional experiences of this type – for example, by realising during a nightmare that the events they are experiencing are only a dream after all. However, some people have lucid dreams quite regularly and even deliberately explore them. Indeed, they have found that the world they experience in lucid dreams is usually much more realistic

Many ancient societies believed that the dead should be buried with objects that they may need in the afterlife. In ancient Egyptian graves in the City of the Dead, above, just outside Cairo, for instance, extraordinary collections of household goods have been found. Many Viking burials often contain, in addition, a horn of plenty, top, holding belongings precious to the dead.

and consistent than in normal dreams, and sometimes almost indistinguishable from the ordinary world of waking experience. The main difference is that, within lucid dreams, they can do anything they like and go anywhere they like just by willing it.

Several people have described how, within lucid dreams, they have visited their own bedroom and seen themselves asleep in bed. Here, the centre of consciousness, within the dream body, seems to be directly and explicitly experienced as separate from the physical body.

CLOSE TO DEATH

The intriguing thing is that such states in lucid dreams seem to be almost the same as the out-of-the-body experiences that are relatively common in childhood, and that may occur in adult life under unusual conditions of stress – when someone is close to death, for instance. As in the case of lucid dreams, a number of people have cultivated the ability to travel out-of-the-body more or less at will. Indeed, those who are familiar with both lucid dreams and out-of-the-body experiences have observed that they are almost identical, except for the fact that the out-of-the-body state is entered via dreams in the one case, and directly from the waking state in the other. This seems to indicate that the centre of consciousness experienced in dreams – the dream body – and the centre of consciousness detached from the physical body in out-of-the-body experiences may be of the same nature.

Such experiences may indeed point to the kind of existence that continues after physical death. Numerous people who have nearly died have described how they found themselves outside their physical body – for example, looking down at it from somewhere near the ceiling of a hospital

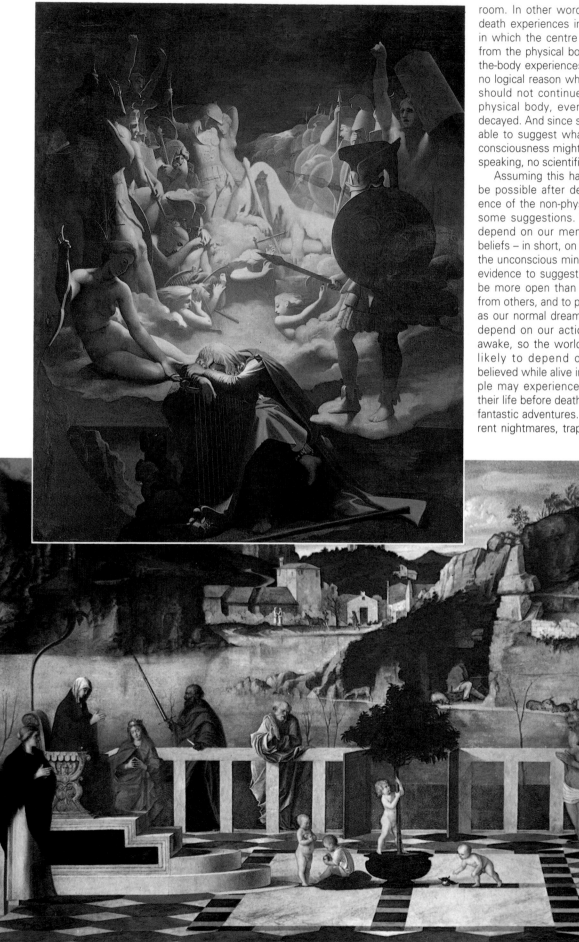

room. In other words, these descriptions of near-death experiences involve an out-of-the-body state in which the centre of consciousness is detached from the physical body, just as it is in other out-of-the-body experiences and in lucid dreams. There is no logical reason why this centre of consciousness should not continue to exist, detached from the physical body, even after the physical body has decayed. And since science has not yet begun to be able to suggest what the nature of this centre of consciousness might be, there is at present, strictly speaking, no scientific objection either.

Assuming this happens, what sort of life might be possible after death? Again, individual experience of the non-physical dream world may give us some suggestions. The kinds of dream we have depend on our memories, hopes, fears, desires, beliefs – in short, on individual personality, including the unconscious mind. There is a certain amount of evidence to suggest that, in dreams, we may also be more open than usual to telepathic influences from others, and to precognitions of the future. Just as our normal dreams reflect our personalities and depend on our actions and beliefs while we are awake, so the world we enter after death seems likely to depend on what we have done and believed while alive in the physical body. Some people may experience a dream-like continuation of their life before death. Some may undergo the most fantastic adventures. Others may suffer from recurrent nightmares, trapped in some form of hell that has been created by their own minds. And others may experience a kind of paradise conjured up by their expectations: Muslims, for example, may tend to find themselves in green gardens with fountains, attended by dancing girls and serving boys, enjoying the pleasures described in Islamic literature. Roman Catholics may encounter St Peter at the Pearly Gates. Possibilities may be limited only by the capacity of the imagination.

FROM THE OTHER SIDE

If imagination governs the afterlife, it need not mean that we will be confined to a personal fantasy world, unable to communicate with others. Although in the absence of the physical body, normal kinds of communication through the physical senses can no longer take place, direct communication of a telepathic nature may be possible both among the departed, as well as between the departed and the living. Some of the communications 'from the other side' picked up by spirit mediums may be of this kind.

Another possibility is that the surviving personality re-enters a physical body and, as it were, wakes up again in the physical world. This taking over the body of a living person would correspond to what has traditionally been referred to as 'possession'. But if the surviving personality were to become associated with an embryo or a newly born baby, then this would amount to what many religious people regard as reincarnation.

In addition to these possibilities, it is also conceivable that, in the kind of dreamlike existence after death, the personality may be open to spiritual influences coming from beyond the realm of the human mind and imagination. As in this world, such influences may lead to a progressive development of the personality, and a greater openness to the life of the spirit.

All this is inevitably a matter of speculation. We cannot find out from experience until we ourselves die. But even then, we are unlikely to obtain an objective view independent of our beliefs and expectations. For what happens to us seems very

The Dream of Ossian, by Jean-Dominique Ingres (1780-1867), left, shows warriors and languorous women summoned from the netherworld by the beauty of the poet's music.

A 16th-century Mogul Indian painting by Ram Das of the Emperor Babur receiving Uzbeck and Rajput envoys in his garden at Agra is shown right. It has been suggested that the nature of the world we enter after death depends upon our own expectations and experiences. For some, it may have all the luxury and comfort depicted in this painting; for others, it may be a dream-like or even nightmarish continuation of their life before death; or it may correspond to the expectations of the afterlife given by organised religion. The nature of the afterlife, in short, may be determined by the imagination of the individual.

An Attic kylix of around 430 BC, left, shows Pluto and Persephone, joint rulers of Hades. According to Greek mythology, it was Pluto's responsibility to supervise the trials and punishment of souls after death.

In the Allegory of Purgatory by Giovanni Bellini (c.1430-1516), far left, the foreground represents a paradise garden with the tree of knowledge in the centre. Justice and punishment are suggested by the figure with the sword.

likely to depend on our own attitudes. In particular, the possibility of continued spiritual development may depend on our openness to this very possibility. Could it be that, if we close our minds to anything that lies beyond, we may condemn ourselves to remain trapped indefinitely within our present fears and limitations?

❝ THE CENTRE OF CONSCIOUSNESS WHICH WAS IN EXISTENCE BEFORE DEATH DOES NOT CEASE TO BE IN EXISTENCE AFTER DEATH AND... THE EXPERIENCE OF THIS CENTRE AFTER DEATH HAS THE SAME KIND OF CONTINUITY WITH ITS EXPERIENCE BEFORE DEATH AS THAT OF A MAN WHO SLEEPS FOR A WHILE AND WAKES AGAIN. **❞**

W. R. MATTHEWS, PSYCHICAL RESEARCH AND THEOLOGY

MESSAGES FROM BEYOND

A GROUP OF DEDICATED PSYCHICAL RESEARCHERS PLANNED – AFTER THEIR DEATHS – TO SEND EVIDENCE OF THEIR SURVIVAL TO CERTAIN CHOSEN MEDIUMS

An ardent and vociferous believer in the afterlife, Frederic Myers – classical scholar and founder member of the Society for Psychical Research (SPR) – wished passionately to communicate his belief to others. But to judge from an impressive body of evidence, he never desired it more than after his death in 1901. For the following 30 years, the SPR collected and collated over 2,000 automatic scripts, said to be transmitted from Myers and other deceased members of the Society, through the mediumship of several ladies. These messages seem to have been specifically designed to prove to the living the reality of the afterlife.

What have become known as the 'cross-correspondences' do indeed seem to point to some kind

Frederic Myers, above, respected founder member of Britain's Society for Psychical Research, is said to have tried to prove his survival after death to his living friends and colleagues. He supposedly sent messages through various mediums, in widely separated parts of the world, by means of automatic writing, which he had studied intensively in life. The fragment, above left, is in a hand markedly different from the normal script of the medium who produced it.

of intelligent communication between the living and the dead – arranged in such a way as to confound critics. Whoever thought up the system, on this or the other side of the veil, was very ingenious.

Apart from Myers, the purported spirit communicators were Edmund Grundy (died 1888) and Professor Henry Sidgwick (died 1900). The mediums included 'Mrs Holland' (pseudonym of Mrs Alice Flemming), who lived in India and was the sister of Rudyard Kipling; 'Mrs Willett' (pseudonym of Mrs Combe-Tennant), who lived in London; Mrs A. W. Verrall, a teacher of Classics at Cambridge University, England; her daughter, Helen (later, Mrs W.H. Slater); and the famous American trance medium, Leonora Piper of Boston, Massachusetts.

A COMPLEX PLAN

The purpose and design of the cross-correspondences is bold yet at the same time complex. But it is this very complexity that gives them their unique air of authenticity. The plan, as far as it can be understood, was as follows.

After Myers' death, he and his deceased colleagues from the SPR worked out a system by which fragments of automatic script, meaningless in themselves, would be transmitted through different mediums in widely separated parts of the world. When brought together, however, they would prove to make sense. To make understanding them all the more difficult, the fragments were to be in Greek or Latin, or contain allusions – sometimes fragmentary in themselves – to classical works. In Myers' words, as dictated to Mrs Verrall: 'Record the bits and, when fitted, they will make the whole . . . I will give the words between you neither alone can read, but together they will give the clue he wants.'

The classical references were way beyond the scope of most of the mediums, except for the Verralls, showing that the scripts were not the products of their own minds. The fact that the fragments were unintelligible to the mediums themselves also ruled out the possibility of joint telepathic composition by them.

It seems that Myers thought of this plan once he had the ultimate personal proof of the afterlife. None of the thoughts he recorded during his earthly life even hints at this scheme. But at least he knew how to set about proving his point since, as an ex-president of the SPR, he knew which mediums were genuine and competent automatic 'scribes'.

The various automatists – in England, India and the United States – were instructed to send their apparently meaningless scripts to certain investigators, whose addresses were supplied. Each piece of automatic script was to be carefully dated and, if possible, witnessed.

An example of what H. F. Saltmarsh, in *Evidence of Personal Survival,* calls a 'simple' cross-correspondence is as follows. Mrs Piper, in America, heard – in a trance state – a word she first took to be *sanatos.* She then corrected herself (she was speaking her impressions out loud to be written down) to *tanatos.* That was on 17 April 1907. Later in the month, the word came through as *thanatos,* and on another occasion was repeated three times. On 7 May, the whole phrase 'I want to

Leonora Piper, below, was one of the most celebrated mediums of modern times. Several of the distinguished researchers who studied her, including Myers, allegedly communicated through her after their deaths.

say *thanatos'* came through. Mrs Piper did not recognise the word as being the Greek for 'death', however.

Meanwhile, on 16 April 1907, Mrs Holland in India received a curious opening phrase in her automatic script: 'Maurice Morris Mors. And with that the shadow of death fell on his limbs.' The two names seemed to be an attempt to get to the word *mors* – Latin for 'death'.

SYMBOL OF DEATH

On 29 April 1907, Mrs Verrall – in Cambridge – received this cryptic communication: 'Warmed both hands before the fire of life. It fades and I am ready to depart.' Then her hand drew what she took to be the Greek capital letter *delta* (a triangle). Next came these disjointed phrases: 'Give lilies with full hands [in Latin] . . . Come away, Come away, *Pallida mors* [Latin, meaning 'pale death'].

There are several allusions to death here: apparently, Mrs Verrall had always seen *delta* as a symbol for death; the 'lilies' quotation is a distortion of a passage in the *Aeneid,* where the early death of Marcellus is foretold; and 'Come away... ' is from the song in Shakespeare's *Twelfth Night* that begins: 'Come away, come away, death.' (The first passage, 'Warmed both hands... ', is a slightly altered quotation from a poem by W. S. Landor.)

So it was that three automatists, in three countries and in three languages, received both straightforward and allusive references to the subject of

PERSPECTIVES
LITERARY PROOF

Myers tried to send quotations from the poem The Pied Piper of Hamelin, *illustrated below, by Robert Browning, above.*

One of the most famous of the cross-correspondences has been labelled the 'Hope, star and Browning' case. In January 1907, one of the communicators (unidentified) proposed – through the medium Mrs Verrall – an experiment. The cryptic message read as follows: 'An anagram would be better. Tell him that – rats, star, tars and so on...'

A few days later, Mrs Verrall received a script, beginning:

'*Aster* [Latin for 'star'] *Teras* [Greek for 'wonder' or 'sign'] . . . The very wings of her. A WINGED DESIRE . . . the hope that leaves the earth for the sky – *Abt Vogler* . . . '

Mrs Verrall recognised these as fragments from poems of Robert Browning: *Abt Vogler* and *The Ring and the Book.* Within a week, Mrs Verrall's daughter Helen also produced an automatic script that included drawings of a bird, star and crescent moon, and verbal references to songbirds.

On 11 February, Mrs Piper had a sitting with J. Piddington, a member of the Society for Psychical Research. Myers 'came through' and said he had previously communicated something of interest to Mrs Verrall. 'I referred to Hope and Browning . . . I also said Star.'

The investigators noted that 'hope' had been emphasized by the very fact that, in the

quotation, it had been substituted for another word: the quotation should have read 'the passion that left the ground . . .' and not 'the hope that leaves . . . ' Mrs Verrall, who knew her Browning, had remarked after reading through her script; 'I wondered why the silly thing said "hope".'

There was now a clear correspondence between the 'hope, star and Browning' reference of Mrs Piper and the texts of the elder and younger Verrall ladies. Mrs Verrall told her daughter that there had been such a correspondence; but, in order not to influence her script, she referred not to 'hope, star and Browning' but to 'virtue, Mars (the planet) and Keats'. Two days later, Miss Verrall produced another script that included the phrase: 'a star above it all rats everywhere in Hamelin town'. This was a clear reference to the poem *The Pied Piper of Hamelin* – written by Browning.

Now, Frederick Myers had an extensive knowledge of the works of Browning, and had always expressed a sympathy with many of the poet's aspirations and ideals. So perhaps it was natural that his disembodied mind should turn to his old literary favourites when trying to prove his continued existence to those left on earth.

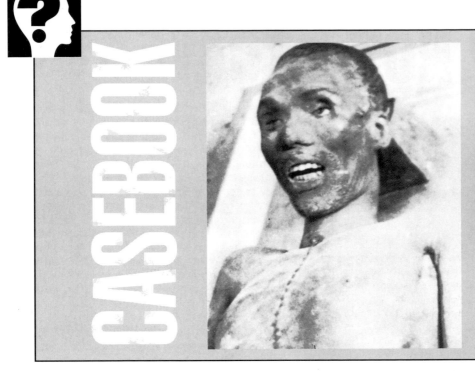

A LEGEND IN THE MAKING

At the end of 1980, in the ancient city of Kano in northern Nigeria, state troops were called in to quell a riot caused by the followers of a heretical Muslim cult, led by the self-styled prophet Muhammadu Marwa (or Maitatsine, as he was also known). Marwa established his headquarters in Kano during the 1960s and thereafter he is said to have attracted some 10,000 followers. Tension between his sect and the orthodox Muslims exploded into a riot in December 1980, during which as many as 8,000 people were killed, including Marwa himself.

At first, Marwa was buried in the bare earth in a shallow grave; but three weeks later the Governor gave orders that his body, *left*, be exhumed and placed on ice at the city mortuary. Rumour soon spread among the people of Kano that Marwa's body was miraculously incorruptible.

So what are the hypotheses most frequently put forward as alternatives to the idea of a miracle? Various kinds of embalming can safely be ignored, since in most fully authenticated cases it is clear from medical examination that no preservatives have been used and none of the viscera removed. Some bodies, however, like that of St Francis Xavier, did have internal organs removed for use as holy relics. Indeed, the incorruptible state was discovered only when the tomb was first opened to take such relics.

HOLY RELICS

Joan Cruz, author of *The Incorruptibles*, outlined three categories of preserved bodies: those preserved deliberately; the accidentally or naturally preserved; and true incorruptibles. Those that fit into the second category show effects no less wonderful for having a mundane explanation; and both Father Thurston and Cruz cite many places that have reputations for preserving human bodies (not always in a mummified form). Cruz, for instance, mentions the discovery of a natural mummy in a mountain cave in Chile in 1954, thought to be the body of a boy who had been drugged and left there to freeze as a sacrifice about 500 years previously. Bodies of Iron Age people have also been found perfectly preserved in peat bogs, but they are greatly discoloured by natural chemical processes. Preservations in alcohol, formaldehyde, honey, rum, sand, salt, and many other unusual compounds – including guano – have been known too; but such bodies are not true incorruptibles.

Certain sites have also been deliberately chosen as burial grounds because their natural conditions delay the onset or acceleration of decomposition. The Capuchin catacombs of Palermo and Malta are famous for their gruesome specimens, of which one 19th-century travel writer wrote: 'They are all dressed in the clothes they usually wore... the skin and muscles become as dry and hard as a piece of stockfish, and though many of them have been here upwards of 250 years, yet none are reduced to

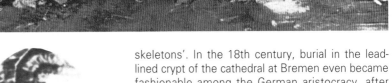

The young lady of Loulan, centre, was unearthed in China's remote Xinjiang province in 1981. Experts claim that this 6470-year-old mummy is the oldest in the world.

Julia Buccola Petta, above, was exhumed in 1927 – six years after her death. Her preservation was believed to be miraculous. This photograph was taken to be made into the plaque that now adorns her grave in Mount Carmel Cemetery, Hillside, Illinois.

skeletons'. In the 18th century, burial in the lead-lined crypt of the cathedral at Bremen even became fashionable among the German aristocracy, after the discover of the astonishingly well-preserved body of a workman who had met with a fatal accident down there several years earlier.

DRY AIR

The vaults under St Michan's Church in Dublin have similar qualities. A survey of the church in 1901 mentions, for instance, the striking example of 'a pathetic baby corpse, from whose whole plump wrists still hang the faded white ribbons of its funeral', with the date 1679 on the coffin. The preservative effect is believed to be caused by the extreme dryness of the air and its freedom from dust – conditions that also prevail in the Russian necropolis at Kiev, in which a large number of withered bodies lie in their open coffins (now covered with glass).

Radiation, meanwhile, was suggested as the preserving agent of the 250-year-old desiccated bodies found in the Wasserburg Somersdorf Castle, at Mittelfranken, Germany. But even though tiny amounts of radiation have been detected in the castle tombs, this does not explain all odd mummifications, nor truly intact bodies.

A further consideration is the curious natural process known as *saponification*. In this, as the name suggests, the body tissues are turned into an ammoniacal soap beneath a toughened outer skin. This soap-like substance is called *adipocere* (from the Latin *adeps* for fat, and *cera*, meaning wax) – or *gras de cadavre* (French, for 'corpse fat'). It is caused by burial in damp soil in the proximity of putrefaction. Why it develops in some cases and not others is unknown. A certain Monsieur Thouret, who was commissioned to clear the cemetery of the Church of the Holy Innocents in Paris, in 1785, found that many bodies had converted to adipocere, and described them as follows:

'The bodies themselves, having lost nothing of their bulk, and appearing to be wrapped in their shrouds, like so many larvae, had, to all seeming, suffered no decay. On tearing apart the grave-clothes which enveloped them, the only change one noticed consisted in this, that they had been converted into a flabby mass or substance, the whiteness of which stood out the more clearly in contrast to the blackness in which they lay'.

Saponification is unusual but not rare: there is a saponified soldier from the United States Civil War period in the Smithsonian Museum, Washington, for instance. It even seems likely that a few cases of alleged incorruption might have been due to adipocere. The exhumation of Blessed Marie de Sainte-Euphrasie Pelletier, who died in 1868, seems to support this idea. Thirty-five years later, her lead coffin was opened to reveal the recognisable features of the foundress of the Good Shepherd Nuns.

A grisly display of dead Capuchin monks hangs, like so many broken dolls, in the catacombs in Palermo, Sicily, below. Most bodies left exposed to the air decay approximately eight times faster than those that are buried – but the air in these catacombs has the peculiar property of drying out the bodies and turning them into natural mummies.

'The mouth was slightly open, the eyes shut, the eyelashes intact,' wrote one examining doctor. Without unclothing the body, he was 'able to ascertain that the chest, the abdomen, the thighs and the legs were covered with a skin like that of a mummy, under which was a mass of *gras de cadavre,* resulting from the saponification of the tissues underneath'.

 FOR THOSE OF US WHO HAVE LOVED AND ADMIRED CERTAIN OF THESE SAINTS, IT IS A COMFORT OF SORTS TO KNOW THAT ... THEIR ACTUAL BODIES, WHICH WILL ONE DAY BE MADE GLORIOUS, ARE STILL PRESENT AMONG US. ▰▰

JOAN CRUZ

True incorruption triumphs over the condition of the body, the circumstances of the burial and the normal processes of decomposition, however. For some reason, a certain body stays intact while others, in the same place, rot into dust. The Catholic Church sees it as a 'divine favour' to a pious soul, although this is not, on its own, enough for beatification (except in the Russian Orthodox Church). Joan Cruz summarises the value of the relics for Catholics as follows: 'For those of us who have loved and admired certain of these saints, it is a comfort of sorts to know that they are not just somewhere in the great realms beyond, but that their actual bodies, which will one day be made glorious, are still present among us'.

SECULAR CASES

But objective researchers are not blessed with such certainty, for they see authenticated cases occurring outside the Catholic Church, and in most cultures. A secular case, typical of the form in which one might encounter it in folklore, was reported in the *News of the World* on 8 May 1977. It concerned Nadja Mattei, who died in Rome in 1965, aged two. Her mother claimed that for 12 years her dead daughter came to her in dreams, begging to be fetched from her coffin. Early in 1977, the authorities granted her request for exhumation, and baby Nadja's body was found to be quite free of putrefaction.

Authenticated true incorruption is very rare; and each story, both in a religious context and outside it, has a similar structure: an incorrupt body, an eerie persistent fragrance, and frequently attendant paranormal phenomena, such as strange lights around the grave or revelation of incorruption through a dream. The universal similarity in these accounts suggests some kind of archetypal event that transcends ordinary reality. The questions it raises, meanwhile, strike to the core of the nature of our physical and spiritual existence, and even the nature of reality itself.

FUTURE LIVES

IF WE CAN BE HYPNOTISED TO RELIVE PAST LIVES, CAN WE ALSO BE HYPNOTISED TO 'SEE' INTO POSSIBLE FUTURE INCARNATIONS?

The discovery by hypnotists that subjects could be taken back to adolescence, childhood, infancy, and even, it was claimed, back into the womb, was followed by regression to alleged previous lives. Ian Wilson's book, *Mind out of Time,* appears to show that one day most, if not all, of such lives may be explicable by what will be seen as normal principles.

But if it is possible to regress subjects into previous lives, and if time is not the simple progression that it normally appears to be, providing 'slips' into the past, should it not then be possible to project hypnotic subjects into *future* lives? Such an idea raises complicated philosophical questions, but there are known experiments that have attempted to progress as well as regress hypnotic subjects.

Early work in this field was carried out by a pioneer of past-life regression, the Frenchman Colonel Albert de Rochas. In the first decade of the 20th century, he progressed no fewer than 10 subjects – all female – into the future, sometimes of their present lives, and sometimes apparently through their deaths into existences yet to begin.

He used a system of 'longitudinal passes' (waving his hand up and down in front of the subjects) to take them into the past and 'transversal passes' (sideways gestures) to return them to the present. By continuing, he also managed to carry them forward by a series of stages to future years.

The subjects seemed, at a subconscious level, eager to please de Rochas by incorporating him into their accounts of the future, his presence being, apparently, the only comfort in singularly unpleasant lives. Details of these future existences seemed to be based largely on fears of what was to come, which the subconscious then dramatised as having already happened.

Dr Rochas began his experiments with Josephine, an 18-year-old servant working at Voiron, whom he regressed normally. After a number of sessions with her, he had occasion to go to Paris in 1904 and renewed experiments with a former subject, Madame Lambert, aged 40. Having regressed her and returned her to the present, he continued the transversal passes under the pretext of waking her more completely, but in reality to find out what would happen. After a time, without questioning her for fear of in some way implanting a suggestion, he asked her to look at herself in a mirror and tell him what colour her hair was. She described it as grizzled, whereas at the time it was still completely black.

After further passes, she found herself growing very feeble and complained that every day she was losing strength. She said she had decided to live with her younger brother who, she was convinced, was going to marry. (Actually, she went on to live alone, not with her brother.) She also saw herself aged 45, looking after an old man in the country and found this tedious.

De Rochas did not dare continue the ageing process without warning the subject, and suggested to her, in her normal state, that he might bring her to the moment of her death, a proposal she vehemently rejected, although she had remembered nothing of either past or future life under hypnosis. Experiments with Madame Lambert were finally discontinued because de Rochas left Paris.

The painting, below, dates from around 1596, is by an anonymous artist and shows scenes from the entire life of Sir Henry Unton, an English aristocrat. According to one theory, our future lives may be similarly laid out, so that in certain circumstances – such as being put into an hypnotic trance – we can see and describe scenes from them.

Back home, he renewed his experiments with Josephine, using the same method to take her into her future, as he had with Madame Lambert. The composite result of seven sessions was as follows. Further progression showed she entered de Rochas' service (later proving true) for six weeks while awaiting a position as a salesgirl at a Grenoble store, Les Galeries Modernes (false). She also gave entirely fictitious details of her lodgings while supposedly working there. She left the store after three months and was asked by de Rochas to return to Voiron for further experiments (false). As she was about to set out, however, she said that her mother died (inconsistent) and she heard no more from de Rochas. At the age of 25, she was living with her parents, having left domestic service three years before. Further passes caused her to show signs of great suffering, writhing in her chair, averting her head, burying her face in her hands, weeping and showing such agony of spirit that her mistress, who was present, was so moved that she withdrew to another room.

Josephine, overwhelmed by grief and shame, went on to reveal that she was now 32 and that two years earlier she had been seduced under promise of marriage by a young farmer whose name she refused to give until later, when she said it was Eugène F. De Rochas. Josephine apparently had a child by Eugène and she saw her seduction as punishment for wrong that she done in a previous, regressed, life.

Progressed to the age of 35, she revealed that her father had died by then but her mother and her child were still alive. At 40, she was still at her village, Manziat, and very sad, her child having died a short time before. (Eugène had married someone else.) Still wretched at 45, she earned her living by cutting out breeches for a tailor. She had no news of her old employers at Voiron, and Louise, her best friend there, had only written three times. In old age, Josephine's sight weakened, owing to her tailoring work, but she forgot some of her miseries. Asked if she would like to know what would happen to her when she left this life, she hesitated and then said, 'Yes'. More transversal passes resulted in her falling back in her chair with an expression of intense suffering, after which she slid to the ground. She was nearly 70 when she 'died'.

A HAPPY RELEASE

Continuing the passes, de Rochas then questioned her about the afterlife. She said she was without suffering, but saw no spirits. She said she had witnessed her own funeral and heard people at it say that her death was a happy release for a poor woman who had nothing to live for. The priest's prayers had meant little to her, but his circling the coffin had driven away evil spirits. She then entered a state of almost complete darkness, lit from time to time by gleams of light in which she saw around her more or less luminous spirits with whom she found she was unable to communicate. She felt a need to reincarnate and signalled her desired entry into her new mother's womb by adopting the familiar foetal position.

 SOME OF DR WAMBACH'S SUBJECTS TOLD OF AN APOCALYPSE, WITH THE GLOBE'S POPULATION REDUCED TO A TWENTIETH OF ITS PRESENT SIZE. INDEED, SUCH WIDESPREAD DISASTERS OCCURRED IN THE 21ST CENTURY THAT, BY THE YEAR 2100, THE EARTH WAS BARREN ... AND WHAT WAS LEFT OF THE POPULATION HAD TO LIVE IN DOMED CITIES, EATING ARTIFICIAL FOODS. //

Her voice then became that of a two-year-old child, called Lili, a contraction of Alice or Elise, daughter of Claude and Françoise. The child, who could not give her surname nor the district in which the family lived, died aged three or four (both ages were given at different sessions). She was not, she said, completely 'in' her body, and saw around her

spirits, both good and bad. After this particular death, she wandered happily in space, no longer seeing the Earth but shining spirits who did not speak to her, and among whom could not recognise her parents or friends. She remembered her past experiences little by little but could not account for the purpose of all these incarnations.

Nevertheless, she entered yet another existence as Marie, daughter of Edmond and Rosalie Baudin, bootsellers at St Germain-du-Mont-Or. She was 16 in 1970, wrote her name – but in Josephine's handwriting – and lived in a France that was a republic.

De Rochas found, to his surprise, that at his third session with Josephine, longitudinal passes took her into the future, not the past, and transversal passes brought her back again. Yet, at other sessions, his original method had its expected results. After his final sitting with her, he took her through all her previous prophecies and, by pressing her forehead, he was able to remind her of them.

A certain Mademoiselle Mayo, aged 18 – another of de Rochas' subjects – could not see beyond

Albert de Rochas' first hypnotic subject, Josephine, an 18-year-old domestic servant, lived in Voiron, France, above, in the first years of the 20th century. Under hypnosis, she seemed troubled by a deep sense of insecurity about what the future held.

her twentieth year. She foresaw a future in which she left home at Aix with sadness at the age of 19. She had gone with her step-father to a land where the inhabitants were black and naked, and she had glimpses of being in a house near a railway station, the name of which she could not read. Later, in the same country, she saw herself playing at a theatre, but in what production she could not say. The girl did, in fact, leave her home-town of Aix in obscure circumstances, telling her friends nothing. Indeed, de Rochas commented that her vision of the future so frightened her that she vehemently refused to reveal it entirely.

Sixteen-year-old Juliette, an artists' model, saw her future life in far more detail, and told de Rochas, advancing three years, how she had previously left Grenoble for Geneva because her step-father could find no work, and had now started to pose for a sculptor by the name of Drouet. She even described what she ate and gave specific information about her daily routine. Eventually, however, she caught cold whilst posing and had to give it up, moving to Nice where she died from a serious illness at only 25. Reborn into a well-to-do family, she said she then became Emile Chaumette, and was eventually ordained as a priest. When de Rochas tried to follow up details of the life of Juliette, however, he found that she did indeed leave Grenoble with her mother, but was unable to make other details tally to any meaningful degree.

INTO THE FUTURE

Dr Helen Wambach, an American, began her researches into future lives in the early 1980s, and has since offered workshops at which subjects can be progressed to the years 2100 or 2300. The intention was not specifically to investigate individual cases, but rather to assemble a compendium of rather mundane facts on ordinary people. She had discovered that it was not constructive to ask questions that might be disturbing or damaging to the subject's self-awareness. Indeed, emotive questions such as 'how did you die?' were found to block the flow of responses.

Usually, she chose a year and a date which would most likely be remembered, such as a birthday. The replies dealt with everyday matters, children, credit card worries, or career plans; and the same pattern was followed year after year. Then the pattern would change. After being progressed forward several decades, many subjects reported being in a blissful state of lightness, and floating freely. Dr Wambach's view was that the subjects were reporting an existence between incarnations. Other subjects, progressed to the same period, gave a very dismal account of life then. After correlating the accumulated reports, Dr Wambach came to the depressing conclusion that some universal cataclysm had overtaken the planet. Some 'souls' were able to find bodies to inhabit, while others floated in limbo, or perhaps faded from existence altogether.

In the hypnosis technique used by Dr Wambach, subjects are asked to visualise their own front doors as clearly as possible. They are then taken, in imagination, to the rooftop, and asked to view the surroundings. Then they are to imagine themselves

Few people view the future with equanimity. Films like **Metropolis,** **above,** *which was made in 1927,* **and Soylent Green, below,** *made in 1973, share the vision of a soulless future where individualism is ruthlessly suppressed. Similarly, future 'lives', described under hypnosis, often seem to be dramatisations of our deepest fears and anxieties.*

feeling light, and gently taking off, flying swiftly over land to a favourite beach. Wambach would next ask them to visualise a white cloud, on which they could relax and ride backwards or forwards in time. Rather than take them to a specific date which might provoke anxieties, she would invite them to choose a period in the past or future which they found pleasant.

Some of Dr Wambach's subjects (as reported in *Mass Dreams of the Future*) told of an apocalypse, with the globe's population reduced to a twentieth of its present size. Indeed, such widespread disasters occurred in the twenty-first century that, by the year 2100, Earth was barren, the soil poisoned and what was left of the population had to live in domed cities, eating artificial foods. More happily, progressions to the year 2300 have revealed that our planet seems to regenerate itself: there are fresh vegetables again, and the population had doubled, re-colonising not just this planet, but others in the solar system as well.

GOLDBERG'S VARIATIONS

Curiously, another hypnotherapist, Dr Bruce Goldberg, conducting research along similar lines, found that his subjects also reported a future global disaster – but not until the 25th century. In his book, *Past Lives, Future Lives,* the dossier of blessings and calamities awaiting future generations includes information pills, geographical changes, and underwater cities.

As a public test of the validity of hypnotic progression, on 2 February 1981, Dr Goldberg put a Baltimore newsreader, Harry Martin, into hypnosis, and then asked him to read the news for the following week. Checking a week later with the actual newscasts, there were a number of notable successes, a detailed description of a road accident being the most remarkable. Further experiments took Harry Martin into a future life in the 22nd century, where he discovered he was employed as a researcher into thought transference, working with 300 other people in a solar-powered glass pyramid. But, of course, only when the requisite time has elapsed can such claims possibly be substantiated.

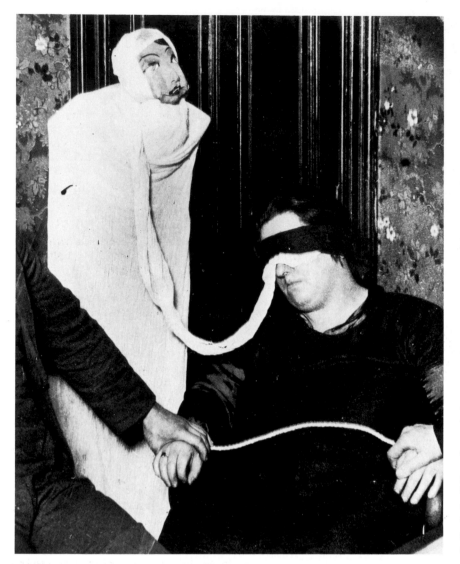

'It is my wish that this takes place for the sake of my little girl,' the materialisation of Mrs Woodcock told the couple. A year later, they were married. At a subsequent seance, a further materialisation of the dead woman told the newly-weds how happy she was they had complied with her wishes.

This touching story of true love was later recounted by Vincent Woodcock in court when he appeared as a witness for the defence in an astonishing trial at London's Old Bailey. In the dock was the medium whose astonishing psychic powers had made possible his wife's return from the spirit world: Helen Duncan.

BACK FROM THE DEAD

Helen Duncan had been born in Scotland in 1898. She married at the age of 20, and her psychic talents were much in demand in the 1930s and 1940s, when she travelled around the country, holding seances in private homes and Spiritualist churches. She convinced thousands of people that the dead could return in physical form. But there were also sceptics who believed Helen Duncan's materialisations were in fact produced by trickery. She was said to have a spirit child, 'Peggy', who played an important role in her seances. But, in a court case in Edinburgh in May 1933, it was claimed that 'Peggy' was, in reality, nothing other than a woman's undervest that a policewoman succeeded in grabbing during a seance. The medium was found guilty of fraud and fined £10.

However, the verdict did not interfere with her career of mediumship. Indeed, during the Second World War, Helen Duncan's mediumistic powers were much in demand by the relatives of those who had died on active service, and she held many seances in Portsmouth, Hampshire, the home port of the Royal Navy. One of these seances, held on

A SPIRITED DEFENCE

THE CONVICTION OF A LEADING PHYSICAL
MEDIUM ON A CHARGE OF CONSPIRACY CAUSED A
STORM OF PROTEST IN SPIRITUALIST CIRCLES.
WAS HELEN DUNCAN GUILTY OR NOT?

The curtains of the cabinet in the darkened seance room parted and out stepped the figure of a woman. Vincent Woodcock recognised her immediately; it was his dead wife. In all, the young electrical draughtsman from Blackpool was to see the materialised spirit of his wife on 19 occasions during seances given by the medium Helen Duncan; but it was this particular occasion that changed his life.

Vincent Woodcock had brought his wife's sister with him to this seance; and when the spirit of his wife appeared from the curtained cabinet, she asked them both to stand. Then, with difficulty, the materialisation removed her husband's wedding ring and placed it on her sister's wedding finger.

At a seance held at her home in 1933, the physical medium Helen Duncan, shown above and right, produced the materialised form of her spirit guide 'Peggy'. Psychical researcher Harry Price claimed it was constructed out of cheesecloth and a rubber doll. However, reputable witnesses, such as the Glasgow medical officer for health, testified at Mrs Duncan's trial in 1944 to seeing many genuine spirit forms at her regular seances.

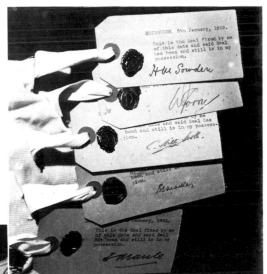

charge was then amended to one of conspiracy. When the case was eventually transferred to the central criminal court at the Old Bailey – where it was dubbed the 'trial of the century' by some newspapers – the Witchcraft Act of 1735 was cited.

Under this ancient act, the defendants were accused of pretending 'to exercise or use a kind of conjuration that through the agency of Helen Duncan spirits of deceased persons should appear to be present....' Other charges were brought under the Larceny Act and they were accused of taking money 'by falsely pretending they were in a position to bring about the appearances of the spirits of deceased persons and that they then, *bona fide*, intended so to do without trickery'.

Spiritualists were dismayed by the use of the Witchcraft Act to bring a prosecution against such a famous medium. Under this Act, it appeared that Helen Duncan could be proved guilty whether or not her powers were genuine.

The prosecution clearly believed Helen Duncan was a fraud, and were not deterred by the absence of any props. During the trial, prosecuting Counsel John Maude produced a long piece of butter muslin and referred repeatedly to the theory put forward by a psychical researcher, Harry Price, that Helen Duncan achieved her results by swallowing muslin and then regurgitating it. Defence witnesses offered to produce a doctor's statement as well as X-rays to show that Mrs Duncan had a perfectly normal stomach, incapable of hiding any props that would produce the effect of materialisation. But these were not admitted in evidence.

Throughout her life, controversy raged as to whether Helen Duncan's ectoplasmic materialisations were genuine or not. In a court case in Edinburgh in 1933, it was alleged that 'Peggy' was in fact a woman's undervest manipulated by Mrs Duncan. A vest was produced in evidence, above and left, with the seals of witnesses who had attended the seance attached.

A ONE-EYED SPIRIT

The trial took place a few months before D-Day and lasted seven days. Numerous witnesses testified to events during Helen Duncan's seances that must have shaken many sceptics. Several people said, for example, they had seen the medium – who weighed all of 22 stone (140 kilograms) – and her tall, thin spirit guide, Albert Stewart, simultaneously. Kathleen McNeill, wife of a Glasgow forgemaster,

19 January 1944, was raided by the police. A plain-clothes policeman who was present blew a whistle to give the signal, and his colleagues burst in. A grab was made at the ectoplasm issuing from the medium and the seance ended abruptly in commotion. Although nothing incriminating was found, Helen Duncan, together with three others who were said to have arranged the seances, Ernest and Elizabeth Homer and Francis Brown, subsequently appeared at Portsmouth magistrates' court on a charge of conspiracy.

At the preliminary hearing, the Portsmouth court was told how Lieutenant R. H. Worth of the Royal Navy had attended Mrs Duncan's seances and suspected fraud. He bought two tickets for 25 shillings (£1.25) each for the night of 19 January and took a policeman with him – War Reserve Cross. Cross made a grab for the ectoplasm, which he believed to be a white sheet, but he was unable to retain it. No sheet was found by the other police officers when they entered the seance room. After the hearing, bail was refused, and as a result the medium was remanded in Holloway prison in London for four days before the case was resumed in Portsmouth.

The prosecution seemed to be uncertain on what charge the four accused should be indicted. On their first appearance at Portsmouth, they were charged under the Vagrancy Act of 1824; but the

> ❚❚ SPIRITUALISTS WERE DISMAYED BY THE USE OF THE WITCHCRAFT ACT TO BRING A PROSECUTION AGAINST SUCH A FAMOUS MEDIUM. UNDER THIS ACT, IT APPEARED THAT HELEN DUNCAN COULD BE PROVED GUILTY WHETHER OR NOT HER POWERS WERE GENUINE. THE PROSECUTION CLEARLY BELIEVED HELEN DUNCAN WAS A FRAUD AND WERE NOT DETERRED BY THE ABSENCE OF PROPS. ❚❚

BACK TO LIFE

A SMALL GIRL, DANGEROUSLY ILL, 'DIED' FOR A QUARTER-OF-AN-HOUR. ACCORDING TO HER OWN ACCOUNT, SHE WENT TO A NEW WORLD IN THE STARS, MET LONG-DEAD RELATIVES AND HAD AN INTERVIEW WITH GOD. HERE, HER FATHER TELLS HER ASTONISHING STORY

Late in the autumn of 1968, Durdana, the younger of my two daughters, then about two-and-a-half-years old, 'died' for around a quarter of an hour. She had been ill for some months, getting progressively worse. She had even begun to become paralysed, and later developed episodes of vomiting and blindness. I was an army doctor in those days, posted to a small unit high in the foothills of the Himalayas. We took Durdana to the military hospital, some miles away, for examination, but investigations proved inconclusive. A suggestion was made that the symptoms might be the after-effects of a viral encephalitis that had claimed the lives of some dozen children in the area some time before.

I was busy in the medical inspection room one morning when my orderly came running to tell me that my wife was calling me – something had happened to baby Durdana.

My living quarters were a large hut in the station compound, adjacent to the inspection room. Durdana had been very bad the night before and, fearing the worst, I hurried home. My wife was in the garden, standing beside the child's cot. A hurried examination revealed no sign of life in the little girl. 'She's gone,' I said. With a look almost of relief, for the child had been in extreme pain, my wife gently lifted the limp little form from the cot and carried her inside. I followed. Certain emergency measures are mandatory under army regulations, and one of my staff, who had followed me from the inspection room, hurried off to get the requisite equipment.

My wife carried the child to our bedroom and laid her down on my bed. After another examination, I began to carry out the prescribed emergency procedures, rather half-heartedly, knowing that they were unlikely to have any effect. While doing so, I found myself repeating, half unconsciously, under my breath: 'Come back my child, come back.'

As a last resort, my wife poured a few more drops of the *nikethamide* – a heart stimulant that we had given Durdana the night before – into the child's mouth. They trickled out of her lifeless mouth and down her cheek. We looked sadly on – and then, to our amazement, the child opened her eyes and, making a wry face, gravely informed us

that the medicine was bitter. Then she closed her eyes again. Quickly, I examined her – and, as I watched her, signs of life began to reappear, albeit very faintly at first.

One day soon afterwards – when Durdana had somewhat recovered from her 'death' and my wife from her shock – mother and daughter were in the garden. 'Where did my little daughter go the other day?' asked my wife. 'Far, far away, to the stars,' came the surprising reply. Now, Durdana was an intelligent and articulate child; and whatever she said had to be taken seriously, or she would become annoyed. 'Indeed,' exclaimed my wife, 'and what did my darling see there?'

'Gardens,' said Durdana.

'And what did she see in these gardens?'

'Apples and grapes and pomegranates.'

'And what else?'

'There were streams; a white stream, a brown stream, a blue stream, and a green stream.'

'And was anyone there?'

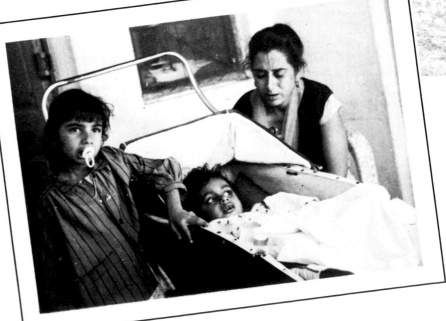

*Durdana's impression – painted in 1980 – of what she saw on her visit to the 'stars' is seen **left**. She found herself in a garden with four streams – white, brown, blue and green in colour. Subtle differences showed Durdana that she could not be on Earth: there appeared to be no Sun, but everything shone with its own faint luminescence, and physical objects seemed to have no substance. Durdana painted the picture, **below**, to show what the scene would look like on Earth.*

*Durdana, aged two-and-a-half years, is pictured **left** with her mother and older sister, after she had 'died' for a quarter-of-an-hour as the result of a neural illness. Once she was well enough to speak, her parents asked her where she had gone during that quarter-hour. 'Far, far away, to the stars,' was Durdana's disconcerting reply.*

'Yes, my grandfather was there, and his mother, and another lady who looked like you.'

My wife was greatly intrigued. 'And what did they say?'

'Grandpa said he was glad to see me, and his mother took me in her lap and kissed me.'

'Then?' 'Then I heard my daddy calling me, "Come back my child, come back." I told Grandpa that Daddy was calling me and I must go back. He said we should have to ask God. So we went to God, and Grandpa told him that I wanted to go back. "Do you want to go back?" God asked me. "Yes," I said, "I must go back. My Daddy is calling me." "All right," said God, "Go." And down, down, down I came from the stars, on to Daddy's bed.'

This was more than interesting. Durdana had indeed 'come to' on my bed – an unusual place for her to find herself, for the children slept or played in

Questioned soon after her experience, Durdana said that she had heard her father's voice calling her home, and had asked God's permission to return to Earth. When asked to describe what God looked like, she could only say 'blue' and drew the impression, left.

their own beds or their mother's, never in mine. And when Durdana regained consciousness, she was in no state to know where she was. But my wife was more interested in Durdana's interview with the Almighty.

'What was God like?' she asked.

'Blue,' came the startling reply.

'But what did he look like?'

'Blue.'

Try as we might, then and later, to get the child to describe God in more detail, she could only repeat that he was 'blue'.

Soon afterwards, we took Durdana to Karachi for treatment at the neuro-surgical department of the Jinnah Post-Graduate Medical Centre. After a complex operation on her skull, Durdana gradually began to recover. I returned to duty, while my wife

stayed in Karachi with the convalescent Durdana. Before they left to rejoin me, they visited several of our relatives and friends in Karachi. While visiting the house of one of my uncles, as they sat chatting over a cup of tea, Durdana started to wander about the room, holding on to pieces of furniture for support – for, extremely weak after illness, she was still unable to stand unaided. Suddenly she called out 'Mummy, Mummy!' My wife ran to her. 'Mummy,' said Durdana excitedly, pointing to an old photograph displayed on a side table, 'this is my grandpa's mother. I met her in the stars. She took me in her lap and kissed me.'

Durdana was quite right. But my grandmother had died long before Durdana was born; only two photographs of her exist, and both are in the possession of my uncle. Durdana was visiting his house for the first time in' her life, and in no way could she have seen this photograph before.

We later moved to London, and Durdana's story began to attract interest from the media. The BBC featured her in a 1980 *Everyman* programme on survival of death and, before the filming began, the producer, Angela Tilby, came to visit us. She admired a number of paintings by Durdana that were hanging on the walls. Durdana had become a gifted landscape painter, and had received many awards and prizes for her work. Mrs Tilby made the interesting suggestion that Durdana should try to paint what she had seen when she was in the stars.

Durdana was later featured on the BBC programme *Pebble Mill at One,* and her paintings of the stars were shown and discussed at some length. The day after the programme had been broadcast, I received a telephone call from a certain Mrs Goldsmith, one of my patients – a very intelligent, well-read German-Jewish woman. She said she had seen Durdana on the television the day before, and expressed the wish to meet my daughter personally and to see her paintings again. It turned out that Mrs Goldsmith had been through an experience of near-death that was very similar to Durdana's. 'I nearly jumped out of my chair when I saw this picture on the television,' she said about one of the paintings. '"My God," I said, "I've been to this place..."'

Durdana stands with her father, below, and shows one of her paintings of the scenes she saw during the time she was apparently dead. One of Durdana's father's patients – a Mrs Goldsmith, above right – saw the paintings when they were featured on the BBC television programme Pebble Mill at One – and immediately recognised the landscapes as those she, too, had seen during a near-death experience.

Listening to her speak, I felt that she seemed a little over-excited – until I realised that what she was trying to tell us was not that she had been to similar gardens in this life, but that she had visited the actual spot that Durdana had painted. It appeared that she had seen more of the place than Durdana had: apparently, I had called Durdana away too soon! Mrs Goldsmith recognised everything that was in Durdana's picture, and also described things that were not in the picture. They sat and talked about what was round the bend in the stream that Durdana had painted, and about the location of the other streams that Durdana had described to her mother.

NEW FREEDOM

But what of Durdana's feelings during her experience? They are strikingly similar to those reported by Mrs Goldsmith, and by many other people who have gone through near-death experiences. She was very happy in the stars, and returned only out of a sense of duty, because I was calling her. She had a feeling of freedom: she felt she was everywhere at once, and could reach wherever she wanted to. There was no source of light, and hence no shadows. Everything was visible through its own luminescence. There was no sound, and there were no animals – at least, she saw none. Physical objects were ethereal images: they seemed to have no substance, no weight. She felt she knew everything and everybody.

I have presented Durdana's story as simply as possible, as it happened. But what does it imply? Where was it that Durdana spent her quarter-hour of 'death'? Durdana herself believes that her experience somehow reflects her own expectations: 'If I had been a Martian, perhaps I would have been sent to a replica of Mars. There, perhaps, God would have appeared red.' And yet Durdana's experience must be more than a dramatisation of her own imagination, for Mrs Goldsmith recognised the very same place.

Such questions remain unanswered. This is merely an account of the experience of one little girl – an experience that is strange, thought-provoking and more than a little awe-inspiring.

VOICES FROM THE DEAD

THE VOICE OF THE CHINESE PHILOSOPHER CONFUCIUS IS SAID TO HAVE BEEN HEARD OVER 2,000 YEARS AFTER HIS DEATH, SPEAKING IN OLD CHINESE. WAS THIS MORE THAN MERE VENTRILOQUISM? WHAT EVIDENCE IS THERE FOR 'DIRECT VOICE' PHENOMENA?

Margery Crandon, a Boston medium of the 1920s, was exposed as a fraud by Harry Houdini, below left, who demonstrated her tricks as part of his stage act. The medium's 'spirit guide' (her dead brother Walter) allegedly left his thumbprint, below, after a seance but this was later proved to be that of a previous sitter, below right. The whorls and ridges (as numbered) can be seen to match exactly.

Jack Webber, right, often produced ectoplasm. He was also said to produce ectoplasmic 'voice boxes' so the dead could speak through them.

John Campbell Sloan could have made a small fortune had he exploited his direct voice mediumship commercially. For, in his presence, the dead were said to speak in their own voices and to hold long conversations with their living relatives and friends. But Sloan, a kindly, ill-educated Scotsman, chose to be a non-professional medium. For 50 years, he gave seances for which he never charged a penny, working instead as a tailor, a Post Office employee, a packer, garagehand and also a newsagent.

Many of the astonishing direct voice seances that Sloan gave were recorded in a best-selling book written by Spiritualist author J. Arthur Findlay, *On the Edge of the Etheric*. In this, Findlay gives an account of the very first seance he attended with Sloan, on 20 September 1918. It took place, as is often the case with direct voice phenomena, in a darkened room.

'Suddenly a voice spoke in front of me. I felt scared. A man sitting next to me said, "Someone wants to speak to you, friend," so I said, "Yes, who are you?" "Your father, Robert Downie Findlay," the voice replied, and then went on to refer to something that only he and I and one other ever knew on earth, and that other, like my father, was some years dead. I was therefore the only living person with any knowledge of what the voice was referring to,' Findlay wrote. He continued:

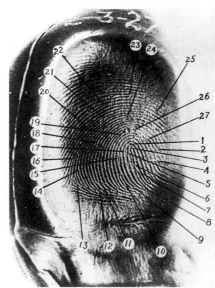

'That was extraordinary enough, but my surprise was heightened when, after my father had finished, another voice gave the name David Kidston, the name of the other person who on earth knew about the subject, and he continued the conversation which my father had begun.'

How do sceptics explain such occurrences? Perhaps the medium was a ventriloquist and had chanced upon the information thought to be known to no one else, they say. But Findlay dismisses such explanations with this answer:

'No spy system, however thorough, no impersonation by the medium or by any accomplices could be responsible for this, and, moreover, I was an entire stranger to everyone present. I did not give my name when I entered the room, I knew no one in that room and no one knew me or anything about me.'

Sloan himself was sometimes able to produce two or three spirit voices simultaneously. On occasions, he went into trance at the start of a seance; on others, he remained conscious and held conversations with the spirit communicators.

Another gifted direct voice medium was Etta Wriedt of Detroit, Michigan, USA. She never went into a trance, nor separated herself from the other sitters by using a cabinet, as many mediums do. Instead, she would remain with the sitters and join in conversations they had with the spirits. If,

George Valiantine, above, was a 'trumpet medium', and accomplished fraud.

however, a foreign language 'came through', she would get out her knitting. She could speak only English.

A British vice-admiral, W. Usborne Moore, also had the opportunity of sitting with Mrs Wriedt when she visited England in the 1920s and testified: 'Frequently two, sometimes three, voices spoke at the same moment in different parts of the circle. It was somewhat confusing.' Of an American seance with the same medium, Moore said: 'I have heard three voices talking at once, one in each ear and one through the trumpet; sometimes two in the trumpet'. These conversations were so realistic, he maintained, that he sometimes forgot that he was talking with 'those whom we ignorantly speak of as "the dead"'.

Another testimony to Etta Wriedt's direct voice mediumship came from the Dowager Duchess of Warwick, who had been one of King Edward VII's mistresses. She first invited the medium to her home because it had been plagued with strange phenomena. On her arrival at Warwick Castle, Mrs Wriedt was shown to her room, while some of her belongings, including a seance trumpet, were left in the hall outside her door. Lady Warwick, while waiting for her guest to appear, ventured to pick up the trumpet and placed it against her ear. Immediately, she heard the characteristic voice of King Edward, deceased, speaking to her, and she found she was able to carry on a conversation with him, partly in German, oddly enough.

Thereafter, the king became a regular and persistent communicator at direct voice seances held at the castle – to such an extent that other communicators could sometimes hardly get a word in edgeways. Finally, in view of her former lover's apparent possessiveness from beyond the grave, Lady Warwick decided to terminate the seances that had been organised with Mrs Wriedt.

Psychically speaking, New York medium, George Valiantine was a late developer. He did not discover his mediumistic powers until he was 43, but soon made something of an impact, particularly with direct voice seances. In 1924, English author, Dennis Bradley, brought Valiantine to England, where he gave seances almost every day for five weeks. The invited guests included 50 prominent people, and around 100 different spirit voices were said to have communicated. Caradoc Evans, the novelist, for instance, spoke to his father in idiomatic Welsh, while other spirits spoke in Russian, German and Spanish.

CONFUCIUS, HE SAY

Probably the most impressive communication of all, however, came at a seance in New York in the late 1920s. Strange and unintelligible voices had been heard previously, and so Dr Neville Whymant, an authority on Chinese history, philosophy and ancient literature, agreed to attend. Dr Whymant did not remain a sceptic for long. First he heard the sound of a flute played in a characteristically Chinese way, then a quiet, almost inaudible voice said 'K'ung-fu-Tzu', which is the Chinese version of the name Confucius, the 6th-century Chinese philosopher and teacher. Few people, except the Chinese, can pronounce it properly. Even so, Dr Whymant did not at first believe it was the famous

Etta Wriedt, left, was one of the most powerful direct voice mediums of all time. Often two or more voices spoke together. On a visit to England, she was invited to Warwick Castle where the Dowager Duchess, below, was experiencing strange phenomena. While showing her to her room, the Duchess picked up Mrs Wriedt's seance trumpet and was astonished to hear her ex-lover King Edward VII, speaking to her partly in German. He later became so persistent that the Duchess gave up attending Mrs Wriedt's seances.

philosopher who was communicating. After all, perhaps it was just someone else speaking his name. But when Dr Whymant began to refer to a passage from Confucius that he believed had been transcribed wrongly, and quoted the first line:

'At once, the words were taken out of my mouth, and the whole passage was recited in Chinese, exactly as it is recorded in the standard works of reference. After a pause of about 15 seconds, the passage was again repeated, this time with certain alterations which gave it new meaning. "Thus read," said the voice, "does not its meaning become plain?" '

Subsequently, after having the opportunity to speak to the voice again, Dr Whymant declared that there were only six Chinese scholars in the world capable of displaying such knowledge of the language and of Confucius, none of whom was in the United States at the time. Dr Whymant also testified to hearing a Sicilian chant at one of Valiantine's seances, and he conversed in Italian with another communicator.

The man who brought Valiantine to England, Dennis Bradley, claimed that Valiantine had apparently passed on his direct voice powers to him; and another regular sitter, an Italian, the Marquis Centurione Scotto, also developed direct voice mediumship.

One of the great British mediums to demonstrate direct voice phenomena was a Welsh miner, Jack Webber, whose powers gradually developed at weekly seances run by his in-laws. He refused to use a cabinet because he knew it would be regarded with suspicion. Instead, he would be tied to a chair, and a red light was turned on at intervals throughout the seance so that sitters could confirm he was still bound. He also allowed infra-red photographs to be taken at some of his seances, to record a number of physical phenomena including levitation, partial materialisation, and the demonstration of direct voice through trumpets.

His powers were recorded by famous healer Harry Edwards in his book *The Mediumship of Jack Webber*, which tells of events recorded over the 14-month period leading up to December 1939, when Webber suddenly died. In that time, more than 4,000 people witnessed Webber's mediumship.

Edwards heard the spirits of men, women and children communicating through Webber's seance trumpets: some spoke in foreign tongues, their messages frequently containing intimate personal information. He also testified on one occasion to hearing two spirit voices singing simultaneously through a single trumpet.

The photographs taken at Webber's seances seem to throw some light on the apparent mechanism of direct voice mediumship. Ectoplasmic shapes appear to connect the medium with the levitated trumpet; and in some of the pictures, small round shapes, about the size of a human heart, are seen to be attached to the small end. These are said to be 'voice boxes' through which the dead are able to speak.

TESTING TIMES

In the United States, one of the most famous physical mediums, 'Margery' (whose real name was Mina) Crandon, allowed some ingenious devices to be used during the investigation of her direct voice mediumship. 'Margery' was married to Dr L. R. G. Crandon, who was for 16 years professor of surgery at Harvard Medical School. Their seances began in 1923, and a variety of physical phenomena soon developed .

One piece of apparatus used to test her powers was developed by Dr Mark Richardson, a Boston resident, and consisted of a U-shaped tube containing water, with floats placed on the surface. 'Margery' had to blow into this through a flexible tube, causing one column of water to rise. She then had to keep her tongue and lips over the mouthpiece throughout the seance to prevent the water returning to its original level. (Witnesses could verify this even in the dark because the floats were luminous.) She did as she was asked, the water level remained as it should, and yet it was found that her regular 'spirit' communicator – her dead brother, Walter Stinson – spoke as loudly as ever.

An even more ingenious piece of equipment was invented by B. K. Thorogood: this was a box comprising seven layers of different materials and containing a large and sensitive microphone. This was closed, padlocked and placed in the seance room in order to record spirit voices. Two wires ran from it to a loudspeaker in another room. People in the adjoining room were able to hear Walter's voice coming out of the loudspeaker, while those in the seance room could hear nothing spoken into the microphone.

Not all these mediums were above suspicion, however. George Valiantine was accused of fraud

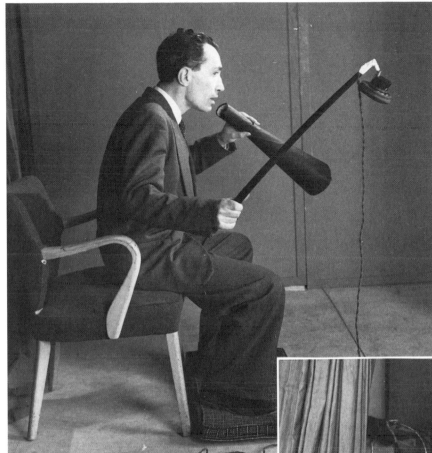

Spiritualism's history. His real name was William George Holroyd Plowright, and he was a small-time crook before he devised a fraudulent mediumistic routine to make money out of gullible people. He even claimed to have made a total of £50,000 from his 'direct voice' seances.

The technique was simple. He used a confederate whose job it was to search people's coats, wallets and handbags after they were safely settled in the seance room. The assistant then conveyed any information thus gleaned to the medium via a sophisticated communication system that came into operation when William Roy placed metal plates on the soles of his shoes on to tacks in the floor that were apparently holding down the carpet. The 'medium' then used a small receiver in his ear. The same device could be clipped to the end of a trumpet so that the confederate could produce one 'spirit voice' while Roy produced another, simultaneously, using a telescopic rod in order to levitate the trumpet.

Roy was exposed as a fraud in 1955 and sold his confession to the *Sunday Pictorial* (now the *Sunday Mirror*) in 1960. Despite being a self-confessed

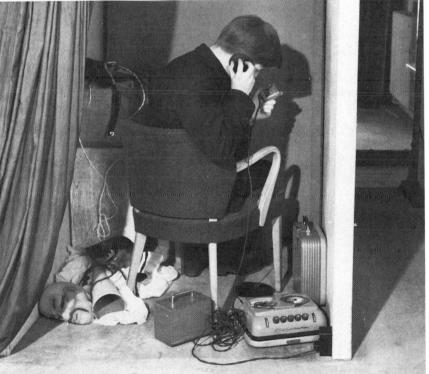

on a number of occasions, and when both he and Mrs Crandon allowed themselves to be investigated by the *Scientific American* – a publication offering $2,500 for a demonstration of objective psychic phenomena – they failed to convince the magazine's committee.

But it was not their direct voice mediumship as such that was to be challenged. Valiantine had produced a series of wax impressions that were said to be the actual thumbprints of famous dead people. He was eventually exposed by Dennis Bradley – the man who had championed him in two previous books – and the damning evidence was published in a third book, *And After*, in which Bradley said the prints 'were produced by Valiantine's big toes, fingers and elbows'.

IDENTICAL PRINTS

'Margery' also ran into trouble with a thumbprint, which was said to have been produced when her dead brother Walter's materialised hand left an impression in wax. In the early 1930s, the Boston Society for Psychical Research showed that the thumbprint was identical to that of Mrs Crandon's dentist, who had been a sitter at her early seances.

Sceptics believe that if these mediums did produce some of their phenomena fraudulently, then it is more than likely that it was all phoney – though how they produced some of their most startling direct voice effects, it is difficult to imagine.

One man who did find a way, and performed successfully for many years, was William Roy – one of the most brilliant and ruthless frauds in

William Roy, top, was a self-confessed fake who claimed to have made £50,000 from his direct voice seances. His confession in 1960 included an exposé of his tricks, such as the use of a confederate in the next room, as shown above. Even so, he later claimed that the confession had been a pack of lies and again set himself up as a medium, this time under the name 'Bill Silver'.

fraud, Roy (who had left the country) returned to Britain in the late 1960s and began giving seances once more, this time using the name Bill Silver. His sitters were numerous, and even included some of The Beatles.

It subsequently transpired that many people who were now attending 'Bill Silver's' seances actually knew he was William Roy, the self-confessed cheat. Yet they now believed that the powers he was demonstrating were genuine. When challenged by a Sunday newspaper, however, he claimed that his earlier published confession was nothing other than 'a pack of lies', published only for the money it would bring him.

DISASTER FORETOLD

THE WORLD WAS STUNNED WHEN THE VAUNTED *R101* AIRSHIP CRASHED IN FLAMES IN 1930. WHAT WAS EQUALLY STARTLING WAS A WARNING OF THE CALAMITY FROM BEYOND THE GRAVE AND SUBSEQUENT CONTACT WITH THE DECEASED PILOT

The R101 is seen as a charred skeleton, below, in the fields near Beauvais, France. Miraculously, its ensign still flies.

Within two days of the disaster, medium Eileen Garrett, right, was 'speaking' to the R101's dead captain.

E ugene Rabouille, a 57-year-old poacher, was distracted from his task of setting rabbit snares by the sound of engines overhead. He looked up into the rain-soaked night and saw a confused image of bright lights and an enormous illuminated shape. It was very low in the sky, moving slowly and falling steadily – and it was heading his way. On it came, the drone of the engines getting louder as it approached. And as Rabouille stood rooted to the spot, the gigantic object suddenly pitched forward, corrected itself, and then slid almost gently into the side of a small hill about 100 yards (90 metres) from where he stood. The next moment, he found himself stretched out on the ground, stunned by shock waves, deafened by noise, and blinded by light.

A wall of flames shot hundreds of feet into the air; and as Rabouille picked himself up, he could hear terrible screams through the fire's roar. He saw, too, in the middle of the inferno, human figures rushing about, alive for a moment or two, but irretrievably lost. Rabouille put his hands to his eyes to shield them from the heat, and from the searing

vision. Then he turned and fled. It was just after 2 a.m. on 5 October 1930.

What Rabouille had witnessed were the final moments of the British airship *R101*, and of the 48 passengers and crew who perished that rainy night near the town of Beauvais, in northern France. He had also seen the event that would crush instantly and irrevocably British faith in the whole idea of rigid airships. It would spark off, too, bitter and lasting recriminations, and provides the backdrop to one of the most curious episodes in the annals of psychic phenomena.

Within two days of the *R101's* sickening destruction, no less a medium than Mrs Eileen Garrett was apparently in touch with the skipper of the enormous craft, Flight-Lieutenant H. Carmichael Irwin. Not only that, it turned out that another airman had actually foretold the end of the *R101* – also from beyond the grave. Three weeks after the calamity, Mrs Garrett found herself in contact again, this time in front of different witnesses, with the airship's dead captain.

PSYCHIC EVIDENCE

Public fascination with these revelations was intense, naturally, as no one knew what had happened during the last few hours on board. The evidence produced by Mrs Garrett was therefore crucial, not only for those who may have wanted to add ammunition to the case for survival after death, but to a question of immediate practical import – the viability of the craft. To gauge how the psychic evidence adds to both debates, it is first necessary to review, in detail, the sad tale of the *R101's* development.

In 1924, the British government had decided that the interests of the Empire could be well served by the construction of a fleet of large passenger airships. Now, the traditional way of going about such an enterprise would have been simply to place an order for a prototype with some suitable

The R100, *is seen,* top, *at rest after her successful flight to Montreal in July 1930.*

It was the genius of Barnes Wallis, above, that contributed so much to the success of the R100.

The R101, *the largest airship ever built at that time,* left, *basks in floodlights at her mooring at Cardington. The hangar that housed her there was the biggest building in the British Empire.*

private firm. However, under a Labour government, there was strong pressure from within its ranks to give a practical demonstration of the merits of state enterprise. In the best spirit of British compromise, the decision was therefore reached that two airships should be built simultaneously, one by the Air Ministry itself and the other by a Vickers subsidiary, the Airship Guarantee Company.

The specifications and standards of performance laid down for the two airships were more or less identical, and they were impressive – more sophisticated even than those for the future *Graf Zeppelin*. They were to be, by a huge margin, the largest airships the world had seen – kept aloft by 5 million cubic feet (140,000 cubic metres) of hydrogen. This would give them a gross lift of 150 tonnes; and with a stipulated maximum weight of 90 tonnes for the airships themselves (unloaded), they would provide a 'useful' lift of 60 tonnes – again far in advance of anything to date.

What this amounted to was a specification for a pair of airships that could transport 100 fare-paying passengers in considerable luxury to the four corners of the globe, and at the respectable cruising speed of 63 miles per hour (100 km/h). This altogether grand vision was by no means as fanciful as it may look in retrospect, however.

The Vickers team set up shop in a disused hangar at Howden, Yorkshire, and over the next five years put together an airship of the highest quality, the *R100*. They accomplished their formidable task in relative peace and quiet, away from the glare of publicity and political meddling. Meanwhile, the Air Ministry team resurrected the wartime airship base at Cardington, near Bedford. There, unlike their rivals, they found themselves as goldfish in a bowl. How great a factor this was in the final débâcle is a matter for speculation, but what finally emerged in a blaze of public anticipation was a majestic flying coffin – the much-vaunted *R101*.

The first in the sorry catalogue of mistakes made at Cardington was probably the worst. Because of the competitive element, it was decided

In a desperate attempt to make the R101 effective, the enormous structure of the doomed craft was split in two to take in an extra gasbag.

were far too heavy. The Howden team, too, experimented with diesel, saw quickly that they were too heavy and reverted to proven Rolls-Royce Condor engines. Such pragmatism was out of the question at Cardington. Considerable publicity had been given to the new diesels and they would stay, overweight or not.

The huge gasbags inside the rigid metal frame (16 of them in all) were held in place by an elaborate system of wiring. But the wiring was such that the bags continually rubbed against the girders and rivets of the framework itself. As bad, or worse even, when the airship rolled (a natural enough occurrence), the valves in the gasbags opened slightly, which meant there was an ever-present risk of highly flammable hydrogen wafting around outside the gasbags, but still inside the body of the airship.

CURIOUS SOLUTIONS

The hurried solutions to these fundamental problems were bizarre – some would say comical even, were it not for the dreadful outcome. There were only two ways of getting more lift: either reduce the weight of the airship or increase the volume of hydrogen. The former was difficult to do to any significant degree (without scrapping the diesel engines), but the latter gave scope to fevered imaginations. Why not simply chop the airship in two and stick an extra bay in the middle? And surely there was an easy way of managing to squeeze more hydrogen into the existing gasbags? Simply loosen the wiring to allow them to expand a little more (and chafe a little more as well). If the gasbags showed an annoying tendency to puncture themselves on bits of the framework, track down the offending projections and stick a pad over them. (Some 4,000 pads were finally fitted).

The immediate results (like the final result) of this kind of folly were roughly what one might have expected. The 'new' R101 was hauled out of the hangar to her mooring mast under perfectly tolerable weather conditions. At once, a gaping hole 140 feet (33 metres) long appeared along the top, where the fabric had merely given way. It was taped up. So was another smaller tear that appeared the next day.

not to pool information with Howden. The design and construction of such advanced airships were bound to throw up problems of both a theoretical and practical nature. Original thinking would be at a premium and there was not a lot of it in the world of British airship design at this time. What the Air Ministry did – deliberately – was to dilute what little there was.

Vickers was in the enviable position of having a truly outstanding designer for the *R100* – Barnes Wallis – who was even then an acknowledged inventive genius and would later become a living legend. During the five years it took to build the two airships, Wallis repeatedly suggested collaboration, but his appeals fell on deaf ears. It was almost as though the Cardington men thought they had nothing to learn from others.

Take the engines, for example. Early on, a newly designed diesel type was adopted because it was marginally safer (from the standpoint of accidental fire) than the conventional petrol type. This should have been weighed against a rather more significant disadvantage of the new diesel engines: they

In defence of the beleaguered men at Cardington, it should be said that they were working under intolerable pressure. In July 1930, the unheralded *R100*, having completed her trials successfully, flew to Montreal and back again a fortnight later. It was rumoured that only the more successful of the two airships would serve as a prototype for future development. To the rattled men at Cardington, it was now vital that the *R101* should demonstrate her superiority quickly. The destination for the maiden flight was India, a longer and more glamorous voyage than the *R100's* to Montreal, and guaranteed to put Cardington back in the limelight.

CALENDAR OF WOE
So we come to the final grim chapter, and to the man who must bear most of the blame for the fiasco that cost his and many other lives – the Air Minister himself, Lord Thomson of Cardington. His devotion to the *R101* project bordered on the fanatical (his choice of title when elevated to the peerage provides a pointer to this). He also combined this passion with unslakable ambition. His sights were set on becoming the next Viceroy of India, and by happy coincidence there was an Imperial Conference in London starting in late October. How better to draw attention to his claim than by descending on the conference, fresh from a round trip to the Subcontinent, aboard his beloved *R101*?

A September departure was impossible. Thomson accepted this, but with ill-disguised resentment. Early October was the latest departure date that would get him to India and back in time to fulfil any of his commitments at the conference. The airship must be ready by the fourth of the month because 'I have made my plans accordingly', he said.

Aside from the fact that the airship was unfit for such a voyage, or even for a Sunday excursion for that matter, there was another hitch. It was essential to have a Certificate of Airworthiness, which could only be issued after the successful completion of exhaustive trials. But a temporary certificate was wangled, with the droll proviso that final speed trials be completed during the journey itself.

At 6.36 p.m. on 4 October, the awesomely beautiful silver craft (for she was that) struggled

Lord Thomson of Cardington, above, had a driving ambition to get the R101 into the air. It only served, however, to hasten its end – and his own death.

The press immediately latched on to the strange aftermath of the disaster, as shown in the headline below.

Spectators, bottom, are dwarfed by the burnt-out wreckage of the 777-foot (237-metre) long airship.

Morning Post

R101: REMARKABLE SEANCE

ONE PENNY

away from her mooring mast. And it was a real struggle. Four tonnes of water (half the ballast) had to be jettisoned in those first moments, just to get airborne. Pitching and rolling, the airship that was, in Lord Thomson's immortal words, 'as safe as a house, except for the millionth chance', crossed low over the lights of London an hour-and-a-half later, with one of the five engines already out of commission. At 8.21 p.m., Cardington received the laconic message: 'Over London. All well. Moderate rain.'

THE LAST MESSAGE
At 9.35 p.m., she reached the Channel at Hastings, still flying low and experiencing worse weather – hard rain and a strong southwesterly wind. Two hours later, she crossed the French coast near Dieppe. At midnight, Cardington received its final wireless message. After reporting the *R101's* position as 15 miles (24 kilometres) south of Abbeville, the message ended on a cosy note: 'After an excellent supper, our distinguished passengers smoked a final cigar, and having sighted the French coast have now gone to bed to rest after the excitement of their leavetaking. All essential services are functioning satisfactorily. The crew have settled down to a watch-keeping routine.'

What seemed to pass unnoticed aboard the airship was her low altitude. It did not go unnoticed by some observers on the ground, however, one of whom was alarmed to see the gigantic craft flying overhead at an estimated 300 feet (90 metres), less than half her own length. That was at about 1 a.m., and he judged her to be moving in the direction of Beauvais.

In the next part of this feature, we find out what happened at the seances held by Eileen Garrett and how the dead captain was heard to speak.

" THERE IS ALSO A NEW TYPE OF ENGINE THEY ARE TRYING OUT WHICH INTERESTS ME. IT IS NOT GOING TO BE A SUCCESS... TELL THEM TO BE CAREFUL. IT IS NOT STABILIZED AS IT SHOULD BE. **"**

CAPTAIN W.G.R. HINCHLIFFE, POSTHUMOUSLY

EVIDENCE FROM THE SEANCE ROOM

WHAT EXACTLY BROUGHT THE _R101_ AIRSHIP TO ITS FIERY END? THE OFFICIAL INQUIRY COULD ONLY GUESS – BUT IT SEEMS TO HAVE IGNORED SOME EXTRAORDINARY TESTIMONY

Reports of the calamity that had befallen the _R101_ began trickling into London and Cardington during the small hours of Sunday morning, 5 October 1930. At first, they were guarded: even as late as 5.30 a.m., Reuters in Paris would go no further than to say that 'alarm' had been caused by an 'unconfirmed report that the airship has blown up'. But this was quickly followed by the death knell: _R101_ HAS EXPLODED IN FLAMES – ONLY SIX SAVED.

The parallel with the sinking of the _Titanic_ was inescapable – a vessel of heroic proportions, the largest and most advanced thing of its kind, safe 'but for the millionth chance', and yet hideously fated on her very first voyage. Public grief was unrestrained on both sides of the Channel.

But even in the midst of that grief, certain starkly insistent questions cried out for answers. How had it happened? Whose fault was it? A special Court of Inquiry was set for 28 October, amid angry

The R101 is seen cruising over the outskirts of London, above, during her first test flight on 15 October 1929. Thousands of sightseers had crowded to see her take to the air.

The captain of the R101 was Flight-Lieutenant H. Carmichael Irwin, above right. The testimony of his spirit voice may well have helped the Court of Inquiry that investigated the tragedy.

rumours that its unspoken function would be to whitewash the Air Ministry in general, and the dead Lord Thomson in particular.

Getting at the truth about the flight, and particularly what happened during those final minutes, proved exceptionally difficult. Fate had been awkward in its selection of survivors. All the passengers were dead; so were all the officers. The only survivors were six lucky crewmen, none of whom was in the main control car (which was crushed) and none of whom was in a position therefore to know precisely how it was that the mighty _R101_ kept her rendezvous with that small hillside outside Beauvais. Put together, their recollections of the final moments added little of importance to what had been seen from the ground

The Court of Inquiry, sitting under the distinguished statesman Sir John Simon, delivered its verdict in April 1931. As the immediate cause of the crash, the Court settled for a sudden loss of gas in one of the forward gasbags. This, if the airship were dangerously low to begin with (as she undoubtedly was), taken in conjunction with a sudden downdraught (which was plausible), would be bound to spell disaster, and was certainly as good a guess as any.

It may well be, however, that what the Court did not consider in evidence held greater significance than what it did. There was considerable testimony that, had it been given credence, would have shed a much clearer light on the disaster and, because of its nature, on issues of vastly greater significance. It was testimony of an extraordinary kind from an extraordinary source – the dead captain of that very airship.

On the afternoon of the Tuesday following the crash, four oddly assorted characters assembled at the National Laboratory of Psychical Research in West London. Harry Price, who had set up the laboratory a few years earlier, was a singular man – wealthy, mercurial, an amateur magician, and a passionate investigator of all sorts of psychic phenomena. And, what was of great importance in the light of what was to follow, he was a savage foe of what he saw as Spiritualist hokum, whether of the deliberately fraudulent variety (which as a magician, he was perfectly equipped to expose) or of the innocent type (in which genuine paranormal experiences, such as telepathy, were wrongly ascribed to 'voices from beyond').

One of Price's guests that day was the celebrated medium Eileen Garrett, a woman of unimpeachable integrity, whose paranormal faculties continually astonished her as much as they did those who witnessed them. Despite the fact that, in trances, she frequently delivered weirdly plausible messages seemingly from beyond the grave, she refused to classify herself as a Spiritualist. And she backed up her strange powers with a disarming eagerness to expose them to the most searching examinations that could be devised by the Harry Prices of this world.

The other principal guest was an Australian journalist, Ian Coster, whom Price had persuaded to sit in on what promised to be a potentially fascinating seance. Sir Arthur Conan Doyle had died a few months earlier. He and Price had wrangled for years

Harry Price, above, arranged the seance at which Flight-Lieutenant Irwin's spirit was first heard.

The bodies of those killed in the disaster lie in state in flag-draped coffins, in Westminster Hall, London, below. Public reaction to the crash was intense; and the French provided full military honours before the bodies were brought across the Channel by two Royal Navy destroyers. An estimated half-million Londoners watched the funeral procession; and world leaders from Hitler to the Pope sent condolences.

– Conan Doyle huffy about Price's acerbic views on Spiritualism, Price discerning a credulity verging on dottiness in the celebrated author.

Conan Doyle had vowed to prove his point in the only way possible – from the afterlife; and Price had arranged the seance with Mrs Garrett to give him his chance. Coster, a sceptic, was there as a witness. Eileen Garrett, as always, did not know the purpose of the seance, nor did she know who Coster was. As far as she knew, it was a straightforward, clinically controlled investigation into her strange psychic talents.

The three of them, along with a skilled shorthand writer, settled down in the darkened room, and Mrs Garrett quickly slipped into a trance. Soon she began to speak, not in her own voice but that of her regular 'control', known as Uvani. He had first manifested himself years before and claimed to be an ancient Oriental whose purpose in establishing himself as a link between Mrs Garrett and departed spirits was to prove the existence of life after death. Sometimes he would relay messages in his own voice, using deep, measured cadences; at other times he would stand aside, as it were, and allow the spirit to communicate directly.

THE UNINVITED SPIRIT

Today, after announcing his presence, Uvani gave Price a few snippets of information from a dead German friend (of whom, incidentally, Price was certain Eileen Garrett was perfectly ignorant), but nothing that excited him. Then, suddenly, Eileen Garrett snapped to attention, became extremely agitated, and tears started rolling down her cheeks. Uvani's voice took on a terrible broken urgency as it spelled out the name I R V I N G or I R W I N. (Flight-Lieutenant H. Carmichael Irwin had captained the *R101*.) Then Uvani's voice was replaced by another, speaking in the first person and doing so in rapid staccato bursts:

'The whole bulk of the dirigible was entirely and absolutely too much for her engine capacity. Engines too heavy. It was this that made me on five occasions have to scuttle back to safety. Useful lift too small.'

The voice kept rising and falling, hysteria barely controlled, and the speed of delivery that of a machine gun. Price and Coster were amazed as a torrent of technical jargon began to tumble from the lips of Eileen Garrett.

'Gross lift computed badly. Inform control panel. And this idea of new elevators totally mad. Elevator jammed. Oil pipe plugged. This exorbitant scheme of carbon and hydrogen is entirely and absolutely wrong.'

There was more, much more, all delivered fiercely at incredible pace. '... Never reached cruising altitude. Same in trials. Too short trials. No one knew the ship properly. Airscrews too small. Fuel injection bad and air pump failed. Cooling system bad. Bore capacity bad . . . Five occasions I have had to scuttle back, three times before starting.

'Not satisfied with feed . . . Weather bad for long flight. Fabric all water-logged and ship's nose down. Impossible to rise. Cannot trim . . . Almost scraped the roofs at Achy. At inquiry to be held later, it will be found that the superstructure of the envelope contained no resilience... The added

middle section was entirely wrong . . . too heavy. . . too much overweighted for the capacity of the engines.'

The monologue petered out at last, and Uvani came back to ring down the curtain on this portion of the astonishing seance.

Three weeks later, on the eve of the Inquiry, there began a sequel to this mystifying occurrence that was every bit as strange. Major Oliver Villiers, a much decorated survivor of aerial scraps over the Western Front, was badly shaken by the *R101* catastrophe. He had lost many friends in the crash, in particular Sir Sefton Brancker, Director of Civil Aviation and Villiers' direct superior at the Air Ministry. Indeed, he had driven Brancker to the airship on the day of departure.

Villiers was entertaining a house-guest who had an interest in Spiritualism, and late one night, when his guest and the rest of the household had gone to bed, he suddenly had an overwhelming impression that Irwin was in the room with him. (The two men had known each other well). Then he heard, mentally, Irwin crying out to him: 'For God's sake, let me talk to you. It's all so ghastly. I must speak to you. I must.' The lament was repeated, then: 'We're all bloody murderers. For God's sake help me to speak with you.' In the morning, Villiers recounted this most disturbing experience to his guest, who promptly arranged a session with the medium Eileen Garrett.

The first of several seances was held on 31 October and, like its successors, it took a significantly different form from the Price-Coster episode.

*In*Focus

THE LAST FEW MINUTES

None of the survivors seemed to know what had caused the *R101* to dive into the ground. One had just dozed off in his bunk when he was jolted awake by the chief coxswain rushing by and shouting: 'We're down lads! We're down!' Another was relaxing over a drink in the specially sealed-off smoking lounge when he felt the airship dip, dip again – and then erupt into flames. Two more, who had been in separate engine cars, were no better informed.

Engine man Joe Binks, however, had glanced out of a window only two minutes before the disaster, and was terrified to see the spire of Beauvais cathedral, 'almost close enough to touch.' He shouted to engineer Bell, another survivor, when the floor seemed to drop away, and then the ship lurched. At the same moment, a message was coming through from the main control car: SLOW. A few moments' silence followed... and then the holocaust.

The Air Ministry clamped down on any news of the crash, yet during the first seance, two days later, 'Irwin' described how he had failed to achieve cruising height: 'Fabric all waterlogged and ship's nose down... '

Three survivors, left, stand near the wreck.

Rather than merely listening to Irwin, Villiers was able to converse freely with him through Mrs Garrett. Moreover, while in the first seance Irwin came through alone, in later seances he was joined by several of his colleagues.

Villiers was not served by shorthand, but he claimed the gift of total recall. This, in conjunction with notes hastily scribbled during the 'conversations', convinced him that the transcripts he made were virtually dead accurate. They make absorbing reading, and a short extract from the first one will give their flavour:

Villiers: Now try to tell me all that happened on Saturday and Sunday.

Irwin: She was too heavy by several tons. Too amateurish in construction. Envelope and girders not of sufficiently sound material.

Villiers: Wait a minute, old boy. Let's start at the beginning.

Irwin: Well, during the afternoon before starting, I noticed that the gas indicator was going up and down, which showed there was a leakage or escape which I could not stop or rectify any time around the valves.

Villiers: Try to explain a bit more. I don't quite understand.

Irwin: The goldbeater skins are too porous, and not strong enough. And the constant movement of the gasbags, acting like bellows, is constantly causing internal pressure of the gas, which causes a leakage of the valves. I told the chief engineer of this. I then knew we were almost doomed. Then later on, the meteorological charts came in, and Scottie and Johnnie (fellow officers) and I had a

consultation. Owing to the trouble of the gas, we knew that our only chance was to leave on the scheduled time. The weather forecast was no good. But we decided that we might cross the Channel and tie up at Le Bourget before the bad weather came. We three were absolutely scared stiff. And Scottie said to us: 'Look here, we are in for it – but for God's sake, let's smile like damned Cheshire cats as we go on board, and leave England with a clean pair of heels.'

Price and Villiers did not know one another, nor were they aware of each other's seances with Eileen Garrett. They therefore arrived independently at the conclusion that the 'evidence' they had should be placed before Sir John Simon. (Price also informed the Air Ministry). Neither the Court of Inquiry nor the Ministry was prepared to accept that these unusual happenings contributed to an understanding of the *R101* tragedy, however.

> **"** HE [VILLIERS]… WENT
>
> UNASHAMEDLY FOR THE PREMISE
>
> THAT HE WAS COMMUNICATING
>
> WITH DEAD FRIENDS, WITHOUT
>
> A DOUBT IN HIS MIND. **"**
>
> **JOHN G. FULLER,**
>
> **THE AIRMEN WHO WOULD NOT DIE**

The *R101* affair is a classic of its kind for two reasons. Firstly, the messages purporting to come from Captain Irwin contained information about a matter of widespread general interest, and were couched in technical language. Everyone wanted to know what had happened to cause the catastrophe, and many were in a position to have informed opinions. Moreover, the official verdict was not particularly convincing – composed as it was of a fair bit of speculation wrapped up in careful qualification (necessarily, since there was not much hard evidence to go on). Someone really well informed about airships in general, and the *R101* project in particular, just might come to the conclusion that Irwin's post-mortem account, although conflicting with the official verdict, had more than a ring of truth. This, by itself, would not have been conclusive, but it may have provided undeniably strong circumstantial evidence for spiritual survival.

Secondly, there is little to raise the question of Spiritualism's chronic bugbear – the suspicion of deliberate fraud. There can be no field of investigation where the personal integrity of those 'on trial' looms larger, and therefore comes under closer scrutiny. Yet medium Eileen Garrett went to her grave with an unblemished reputation. Further, the seances were held in circumstances controlled by a world-famous detective of fraudulent mediumship. To arrange a hoax, even had he wanted to, Harry Price would have needed to enlist as fellow-conspirators both Mrs Garrett and Major Villiers, a

The credibility of Eileen Garrett, above, is central to the R101 mystery. She had been in touch with the spirit of the aviator Hinchliffe, who uttered warnings about the airship; had visions of an airship in flames; and received messages from the spirits of those on board the R101 – seen, top, on its initial test flight in October 1929, cruising over St Paul's Cathedral, London.

distinguished and honourable man – and, indeed, several others.

With fraud out of the way, then, the question turns on whether the information said to have come from the dead Captain Irwin is of such a nature that it could have come only from him. Put another way, is there any possible means by which the information that came via Mrs Garrett could have got to her other than by her being in contact – through her guide Uvani – with Captain Irwin's spirit? If not, the case for the survival of the spirit is made – a simple conclusion, but one with profound implications.

Everything hangs on the details of the messages, therefore; and so it is to them that we now turn. The case for accepting the voice as being that of the true Irwin has been presented in considerable detail by John G. Fuller in his book *The Airmen Who Would Not Die*.

None of those present, he explains, knew anything at all about the complexities of airship design or the business of flying one, and so it is impossible that such startlingly specific statements as those made by 'Irwin' – at wild speed and in what was, to those present, a language as foreign as it is to the lay reader today – could have been dredged from the conscious or unconscious mind of any of them. That rules out straightforward telepathy.

One of 'Irwin's' statements was not only highly technical, it referred to something that would not be known outside the inner sanctum of those intimately involved with the airship – the new hydrogen-carbon fuel mix. Another, the reference to Achy

DID THE SPIRITS REALLY SPEAK?

('almost scraped the roofs at Achy'), is just as bewildering. Price tried to find Achy in conventional atlases without success. But when he tracked down a large-scale railway map of the Beauvais area (a map as detailed as the charts Irwin would have carried in the control car), he found it – a tiny hamlet on the railway lines, a few miles north of Beauvais. Where could such a snippet of information have come from, if not from Irwin himself?

Finally, Price had the transcript examined, clause by clause, by an expert from Cardington (who volunteered for the job). Will Charlton – as did other old Cardington hands – professed himself astonished at the technical grasp displayed therein, and by the likelihood of Irwin's account in its essentials. Indeed, Charlton reckoned that no one but Irwin could have been the source of this information – information that explained clearly what had happened during the fateful voyage as against the speculative account in the official report.

SHAKY GROUND

As far as it goes, this sounds pretty convincing. But such evidence begins to fray at the edges somewhat when it is realised that, in Charlton, Price had not found an expert at all – rather, a convinced Spiritualist whose claim to airship expertise rested on the shaky ground of having been in charge of stores and supplies at Cardington. In a review of Fuller's book for *Alpha* magazine in 1980, Archie Jarman, credited by Fuller with knowing more about the subject than any living person, draws attention to some glaring examples of Charlton's ignorance: they are certainly of such a nature as to discredit him as an expert. For example, during one sitting, 'Irwin' made a reference to '*SL8*'. Price had no idea what this meant, and it remained for Charlton to come up with the answer: 'The *SL8* has been verified as the number of a German airship – SL standing for Shuttle Lanz.' In order to track down this morsel of information, Charlton had to comb through the entire record of German airships.

Now, far from being impressive, such a statement is utterly damning from an expert. 'The SL stands for *Schütte Lanz (Schütte,* not 'Shuttle' or 'Shutte' as Fuller variously had it), the German rival airship development before the First World War, one of which was shot down in flames in a celebrated action during a raid on England in 1916 (a mere 14 years previously). Yet Charlton, the expert, had no idea what *SL8* referred to. It is not good enough, and Fuller drives home the point: 'Charlton and his colleagues of Cardington had been strongly impressed with the reference to *SL8*. No one on the staff of Cardington could confirm this designation and number until they had looked it up in the complete records of German airships.'

Furthermore, when Jarman was compiling a report on the affair in the early 1960s, he solicited the opinions of two real experts: Wing-Commander Booth, who had captained the *R100* on the Montreal flight, and Wing-Commander Cave-Brown-Cave, who had been intimately involved in the *R101's* construction.

Wing-Commander Booth spoke for both when he replied: 'I have read the description of the Price-Irwin seance with great care and am of the opinion that the messages received do not assist in any

The official inquiry into the disaster seemed to add little to the account of the great airship's final moments as provided by the poacher, Eugene Rabouille, above, who saw it plough into the ground.

way in determining why the airship *R101* crashed...' Cave-Brown-Cave ended with the crushing comment: 'The observations of Mr Charlton should be totally disregarded.'

Booth's verdict on the Villiers material was to prove even harsher in content: 'I am in complete disagreement with almost every paragraph . . . the conversations are completely out of character, the atmosphere at Cardington is completely wrong, and the technical and handling explanation could not possibly have been messages from anyone with airship experience.' The latter remark is surely true. Just to take one example, at one point, 'Irwin' complained about the gas indicator going up and down. Booth's trenchant reply was: 'No such instruments were fitted.'

That technical inaccuracy is bad enough, but it is mild in comparison with what the officers are said to have had in mind from the moment they set off from Cardington. They supposedly knew that the airship was most probably a dud and that they had no chance of reaching their destination. But they thought they might just manage to creep across the Channel and tie up at Le Bourget. There were only four places on Earth with the facilities to cope with such an immense airship, and Le Bourget assuredly was not one of them.

WHEN ALL WAS LOST

After they had crossed the Channel, according to 'Irwin', they 'knew all was lost'. So what did they do? They opted to press on into a brutal headwind, hoping to make Le Bourget (knowing all was lost), 'and try at all costs some kind of landing'. Surely no sane person would attempt any such thing, especially when there was an obvious alternative?

If the Captain and his close colleagues really were terrified about the way things were going, all they had to do was turn around and, with the wind at their backs, limp home to the safety of Cardington. Sane men do not accept certain death (and commit dozens of their fellows to the same fate) rather than admit that they have been defeated by an impossible task.

Jarman's view is that nothing whatever occurred during the seance that cannot be put down to Eileen Garrett's own subconscious and her telepathic powers. Take the reference to Achy, for instance – at first sight so inexplicable. According to Jarman, who knew Mrs Garrett well, she frequently motored from Calais to Paris and Achy is on that road, clearly signposted. Could not Mrs Garrett have retained the name subconsciously? Since it is more than likely that the *R101* did *not* pass directly over Achy, what else are we to believe?

And while Eileen Garrett certainly knew nothing to speak of about the technicalities of airships, the *R101* was much on her mind even before the crash. She had already had visions of an airship disaster, and had discussed her fears at length with none other than Sir Sefton Brancker – Director of Civil Aviation – just 10 days before the accident.

The supposed secret nature of some of the technical information provided by 'Irwin' can also be explained. The fact is that the design and construction of the *R101* (fuel mix and all) was conducted with about as much secrecy as the building of Concorde. Anyone who cared to do so could have amassed immense technical detail about the airship simply by reading the newspapers. And, of course, the press was full of it during the interval between the crash and the seances. As for the savage indictments that form the burden of all the seances, the Cardington follies had been notorious all along, brought finally to the fore, naturally, by the disaster.

Those attending the seances were probably very well up on all this; and so if we accept that Eileen Garrett had telepathic gifts, we need look no further, suggests Archie Jarman in *The R101 Rises Again*. That is a perfectly reasonable explanation.

But perhaps the final word should be left to Harry Price. In his letter to Sir John Simon, which is, incidentally, couched in the language of a disinterested research scientist, he states that he does not believe that it was the 'spirit' of Irwin present at the seance. Then he continues: 'I must also state that I am convinced that the psychic was not consciously cheating. It is likewise improbable that one woman in a thousand would be capable of delivering, as she did, an account of the flight of an airship... Where such information comes from is a problem that has baffled the world for 2,000 years.'

> **"** I LIVE IN A WORLD FILLED WITH PHENOMENA OF A TRANSCENDENTAL NATURE... I HAVE LEFT THESE PHENOMENA OPEN TO SPECULATION, BUT I SUSPECT THAT THIS FIELD, WHICH IS SURELY DISCREDITED BY THOSE WHO DO NOT EXPERIENCE ITS NATURE, BELONGS TO THE INNER WORKINGS OF WHAT WE CALL MIND, AS YET TO BE EXPLORED. **"**
>
> **EILEEN GARRETT**

Sir Sefton Brancker, above, discussed the problem of the R101 with Eileen Garrett just before the crash.

The giant airship, left, is manoeuvred by ground crew prior to its last flight.

The stark, burnt-out remains of the R101, below, offered few clues to the precise cause of the appalling disaster.

HOUDINI WAS THE GREATEST ESCAPOLOGIST OF ALL TIME – BUT HE IS ALSO FAMED FOR HIS EXPOSURE OF FRAUDULENT MEDIUMS

In 1924, a contest took place in which Harry Houdini, established as the leading stage magician of his era, was for the first and only time defeated. But he did not admit defeat: on the contrary, he claimed to have exposed his opponent – the Spiritualist medium 'Margery' – as a fraud, just as he had exposed so many others. But in this Houdini lied, just as, unfortunately, by then – he had just entered his fifties – he was all too prone to do.

Houdini was born in Wisconsin in the United States in 1874, the son of Hungarian immigrants, Rabbi Samuel Weiss and his wife Cecilia, who had named him Erich. As a teenager, he read the memoirs of Robert-Houdin, the most famous magician of the previous era; and in response to these, resolving to take on his hero's mantle, he adopted the name 'Houdini' and took an act on tour.

However, it was not long before he realised that, in using Houdin's name, he had made something of a mistake – for he was destined to be even greater. It was too late to change his stage name, but by writing *The Unmasking of Robert-Houdin*, he effectively demolished the Frenchman's reputation. Indeed, this gives us a clue to Houdini's own character; for when Maurice Sardina went over the same ground, he realised that, although Houdini had indeed uncovered many of Houdin's weaknesses, he had also been unscrupulous in distorting the facts to fit his case.

UNMASKED BY HOUDINI?

During his lifetime, Harry Houdini became a worldwide household name – principally for his skills in escapology. A German book cover, left, shows Houdini about to free himself from a fearsome array of manacles. He became known, too, for his replicating of Spiritualist phenomena, as illustrated above. Supporters of the Spiritualist movement, however, pointed out that reproducing phenomena by trickery did not necessarily detract from the authenticity of the mediums' manifestations.

Houdini made his name principally as an escapologist, and in that capacity he was supreme. By 1918, he had escaped from just about every form of confinement that ingenuity could devise, and was beginning to look for alternative sources of income – and fame. He had also starred in several films, and thought in terms of film-making as a career. But he had contracts to honour in Britain as an escapologist. He had signed these before the First World War; and in 1920, he arrived to fulfil them. It was then that he realised an old ambition – to meet the creator of Sherlock Holmes.

Sir Arthur Conan Doyle and Houdini took an immediate liking to one another. 'Apart from his amazing courage, he was remarkable for his cheery urbanity in everyday life,' Doyle was to recall after Houdini's death. 'One could not wish a better companion so long as one was with him.' When one was not with him, however, Houdini 'might do and say the most unexpected things' – unexpected, that is, by Doyle, who found it hard to believe that somebody with whom he got on so well could openly despise him behind his back. For, much as he liked Doyle, Houdini thought him hopelessly gullible in his dealings with Spiritualist mediums. At that time, they were flourishing as never before, thanks to the demand for their services created by the deaths of so many loved ones on the Western Front.

On the subject of Spiritualism, Houdini was, at this period in his life, ambivalent. He had been so passionately devoted to his mother that he was to say of her, in the introduction to his book *A Magician Among the Spirits*: 'If God in His infinite wisdom ever sent an angel upon Earth in human form, it was my mother.' After her death in 1913, he longed to communicate with her, and sat with several mediums in the hope that his mother would 'come through'. But she never did – not, at least, in a way that satisfied him, although Lady Doyle maintained that she had brought him a message from her. But there was something that aroused his suspicion – the fact that his mother's alleged spirit addressed him as 'Harry', a name by which she had never called him in life.

Houdini became increasingly interested in 'physical mediums' from a practical point of view: assuming they were fraudulent, how did they produce their materialisations? His magician's imagination was caught by this question: however, for a short time, Doyle seems to have persuaded him that physical mediums were worth investigating, not just to catch them cheating, but to see whether there might indeed be some psychic force involved.

As it happened, the celebrated Marthe Beraud, better known under her pseudonym 'Eva C', was in London being tested by the Society for Psychical Research. On 21 June 1920, Houdini went to a seance where he was able to watch two expert investigators, E.J. Dingwall and W. Baggally, put Eva C through a carefully controlled trial.

Born Erich Weiss, Houdini took on the name of Robert-Houdin, the French conjurer above, in modified form as a mark of esteem.

Sir Arthur Conan Doyle is seen below left with Lady Doyle and their family. The Doyles were committed Spiritualists who believed that Houdini was himself psychic.

Houdini shows, below, how easy it is to fake a spirit photograph, as he apparently communes with Abraham Lincoln.

Eva's speciality was materialising strange – apparently two-dimensional – human forms and faces. She had been doing this at seances for 15 years, carefully monitored and photographed by such experienced psychical researchers as Professor Charles Richet, Baron Schrenck-Nötzing and Dr Gustave Geley. Although her powers were gradually waning – and she had little success in her London trials – Houdini happened to be present on one of her better days, and he wrote an account of the sitting to Doyle the following morning.

Eva C, he said, had been made to drink a cup of coffee and eat some cake. He assumed they wanted 'to fill her up': in fact, it was a precaution against her having swallowed something before the seance – butter muslin, for example – and regurgitating it

as 'ectoplasm'). After she had been undressed, sewn into tights, and her face covered with a veil to make it impossible for her to disgorge objects from anywhere in her body, she manifested 'some froth-like substance, inside of net, 'twas long, about five inches [13 centimetres]'; then 'a white, plaster-looking affair over her right eye', and 'something that looked like a small face, say four inches [10 centimetres] in circumference'. Finally, she 'asked permission to remove something in her mouth, showed her hands empty, and took out what appeared to be a rubberish substance, which she disengaged, and showed us plainly. We held the electric torch, all saw it plainly; when, presto!, it vanished. It was a surprise effect indeed!'

'Doyle would doubtless receive a detailed report later', wrote Houdini, adding: 'I found it highly interesting.' He was certainly a sufficiently experienced magician to realise that there was no ready explanation for the ectoplasmic manifestation he had witnessed. He also hoped to visit W.J Crawford, the Belfast engineer who had thoroughly investigated the mediumistic Goligher family, and especially their most gifted member, the daughter Kathleen.

Houdini seemed impressed by what he had heard of Crawford's investigations. 'It is certainly a wonderful affair,' he wrote to him, 'and there is no telling how far all this may lead.' But as he had to return to the United States, he contented himself with asking Crawford for some of the photographs he had taken showing the ectoplasm that emerged from Kathleen Goligher, and also the effects of her psychokinetic powers.

Not long after he returned to the United States, however, Houdini began to exploit what he regarded as the 'tricks' of such mediums by giving public demonstrations of them. It was a profitable diversion from escapology. Soon, he even emerged as the great scourge of the Spiritualists, taking it upon himself to expose fraudulent mediums up and

Houdini was on friendly terms with many of those whose beliefs he professed to despise – the Conan Doyles and the flamboyant psychical researcher Harry Price, for instance, with whom he kept up a lively correspondence. Surprisingly, some of the mediums whom he exposed as frauds were willing to confess all. Anna Clark Benninghoffer, below, even posed for a satirical photograph with Houdini, the 'scourge of the Spiritualists'. This seems to argue that, whatever else he was, the magician was a man of considerable charisma.

down the country. And when, in 1923, he was invited to write articles on the subject for the *Scientific American*, although commitments prevented him writing them, his suggestion that the journal should sponsor an investigation into mediumship, in which he would assist, was accepted.

The *Scientific American* offered a reward of $2,500 for 'the first physical manifestations of a psychic nature produced under scientific control'. Mrs Mina Crandon, the wife of a Boston surgeon – who, as 'Margery', was to become the most celebrated of American mediums in the period – took up the challenge. Dr William McDougall, professor of psychology at Harvard; Dr Daniel Comstock, a physicist, formerly of the Massachusetts Institute of Technology; Walter Franklin Prince, research officer of the American Society for Psychical Research; and Hereward Carrington, the most experienced of American psychical researchers – all were appointed, along with Houdini, to carry out the investigation. Houdini, however, could not attend the early seances as he was on tour. Later, he was mortified to hear that the *Scientific American*'s nominee as secretary to the committee, J. Malcolm Bird, had decided that Margery's materialisations were genuine, and that she was likely to win the award.

Houdini had been promoting his forthcoming book *A Magician Among the Spirits* by boasting that he could expose any medium as fraudulent, and backing his claim with bets. Of Margery, he told the publisher of the *Scientific American*: 'I will forfeit a thousand dollars if I do not detect if she resorts to trickery.' By this time, Houdini had convinced himself that all materialisations must be fakes, and he now became utterly obsessed with proving that Margery was a fraud.

SABOTAGE

Margery's spirit 'control', or 'guide', was her dead brother Walter (who, apparently, behaved in the spirit world as he had in life – badly). Walter clearly relished the idea of a contest with Houdini, but Houdini's plan was to enclose Margery in a box, made to his specifications by his assistant, James Collins. It looked like an old-fashioned steam bath, with a hole at the top, out of which her head protruded, and holes at either side so that her hands could be held. Hardly had the seance begun when the whole contraption burst apart, as if exploded by a small bomb. And when Margery was re-installed, the voice of Walter accused Houdini of sabotaging the experiment. He had, claimed Walter, interfered with the box in which was the bell that Margery was to try to ring. Sure enough, a small rubber eraser had been inserted, presumably by Houdini, to prevent the bell sounding. Houdini, it seemed, was hardly playing ball.

For the next seance, Houdini and Collins reinforced the lid of the cabinet in which Margery was installed; but, again, Walter came through with his usual flow of words, which the note-taker deemed unprintable: 'Houdini! You – blackguard! You have put a rule in the cabinet.' Sure enough, in the cabinet, which Houdini was supposed to have searched and found empty, there was indeed a telescopic rule. (No doubt, had Margery caused objects to move, she would have been accused of doing so by working the rule with her mouth.)

But even if Margery could have conveyed the ruler to her mouth while her hands remained outside the cabinet, to have used it to move the objects at a distance, and to start the bell ringing in the box, would have been impracticable, as the ruler was only 2 feet (60 centimetres) long. The most plausible explanation was that Houdini had it put in the box as a last resort, in case he could not detect her in more obvious 'tricks'. Indeed, according to one of his biographers, Lindsay Gresham, Houdini's assistant, James Collins, later openly admitted that he had put it in the cabinet himself and had actually been asked to do so.

PHOTOGRAPHIC EVIDENCE

A later biographer of Houdini, the well-known magician (and sceptic) Milbourne Christopher, was to cast doubt on the story on the ground that it had been spread by a man with a grudge against Houdini. In Christopher's opinion, the story of Collins' confession was sheer fiction. Yet Christopher himself also disclosed how, at this time, Houdini had cheated his fellow investigators, and the public. During the seances, Houdini had asked and received permission to take photographs – to discover, he hoped, how Margery played her 'tricks'. He had asked a friend to have prints made from the negatives, saying 'she's the slickest ever.' The prints showed nothing suspicious, but one of them displayed what looked like a halo around Margery's head. As mediums often claimed to be able to impose such effects on negatives, Houdini suppressed the picture, telling his friend that Spiritualists might claim it proved her psychic capabilities, and adding: 'She's a fake – why should I help build up her following?'

Houdini's escapes from handcuffs, chains, ropes and locked containers of all kinds were so spectacular and considered to be so 'impossible' that his skills were widely thought to be paranormal, even diabolical, in origin. The cartoon, right, shows him as the Devil after his 'escape' from Liverpool jail in 1904. He issued a general invitation to the locksmiths, police and even other stage magicians of the world to confine him successfully, but he always escaped. He took up every challenge and took part in every form of entertainment, such as the circus, below, and always emerged the winner. But did he have paranormal powers, or was he simply a particularly well-rehearsed performer?

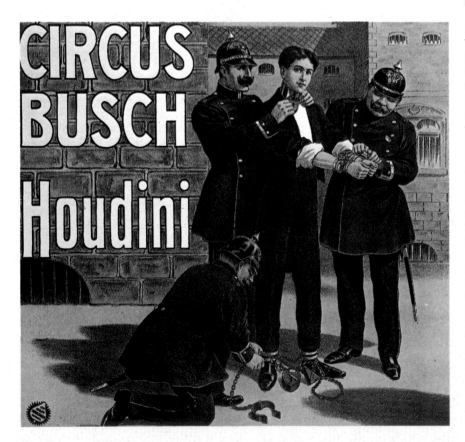

The *Scientific American* committee was divided: Bird and Carrington were sure that Margery had proved her psychic powers; Prince and McDougall thought she must be using trickery, but could not fathom how; Comstock accepted the reality of the phenomena, but refused to endorse them unless they could be explained in terms of electromagnetism. To the irritation of his colleagues on the committee, however, Houdini resumed his tour of the halls, claiming that he had exposed Margery. But his failure had clearly annoyed him; for when given another opportunity to try again a few months later, he accepted.

MAGICAL FEATS

The new chief investigator was Dr Henry McComas, a psychologist at Princeton University. Houdini, who by that time had learned caution, told him to attend a seance and report back what Margery did – 'the lady is subtle and changes her methods like any dextrous sleight-of-hand performer' – so that he would have time to work out how to duplicate her feats. McComas reported that Margery was now performing while enclosed in a glass case. Her feats had been spectacular, including the levitation of objects outside the case. Baffled, Houdini asked for time to decide how he could do what Margery was doing; but before he was ready, McComas had abandoned his investigation and returned to Princeton.

In 1926, an alleged spirit message came through at Conan Doyle's home circle: 'Houdini is doomed, doomed, doomed!' Other Spiritualists reported receiving similar communications. Then, on 24 October that year, one of Houdini's allies in the campaign against mediums was sitting in his room when a picture of Houdini, which the magician had given him, crashed to the floor. 'Maybe,' he wrote anxiously, 'there is something in these psychic phenomena, after all.' A week later, Houdini was dead. 'I knew him well,' said the author Walter Franklin Prince, 'and the world seemed poorer when his big heart and eager brain were stilled.'

MEDIUMS ON TRIAL

WILLI AND RUDI SCHNEIDER BECAME CELEBRATED MEDIUMS DURING THE 1920S AND WERE STRINGENTLY INVESTIGATED BY LEADING PSYCHICAL RESEARCHERS. HOW AUTHENTIC WERE THE PHENOMENA THEY PRODUCED?

In the spring of 1919, rumours began flying around the small Austrian city of Braunau. It was said that spirits were being conjured up in the flat of Herr Josef Schneider. Twenty-five years later, the psychical investigator Harry Price was to write of Braunau as 'a charming frontier old-world village which is famous as the birthplace of three distinguished persons – Adolf Hitler, and Willi and Rudi Schneider, the Austrian physical mediums'.

Willi Schneider is seen below in a state of trance during a seance in Munich in 1922. Two German psychical researchers are acting as controllers.

Josef and Elise Schneider had 12 children altogether, nine boys and three girls, but only six boys survived: Karl, Hans, Fritz, Willi, Franz and Rudi.

Rudi, the youngest, was born on 27 July 1908. His parents, disappointed that he was a boy, put him in girls' clothing, curled his hair and even called him 'Rudolfine' for a time. He seems to have survived the ordeal, taking up the traditionally boyish pursuit of football and showing a special interest in

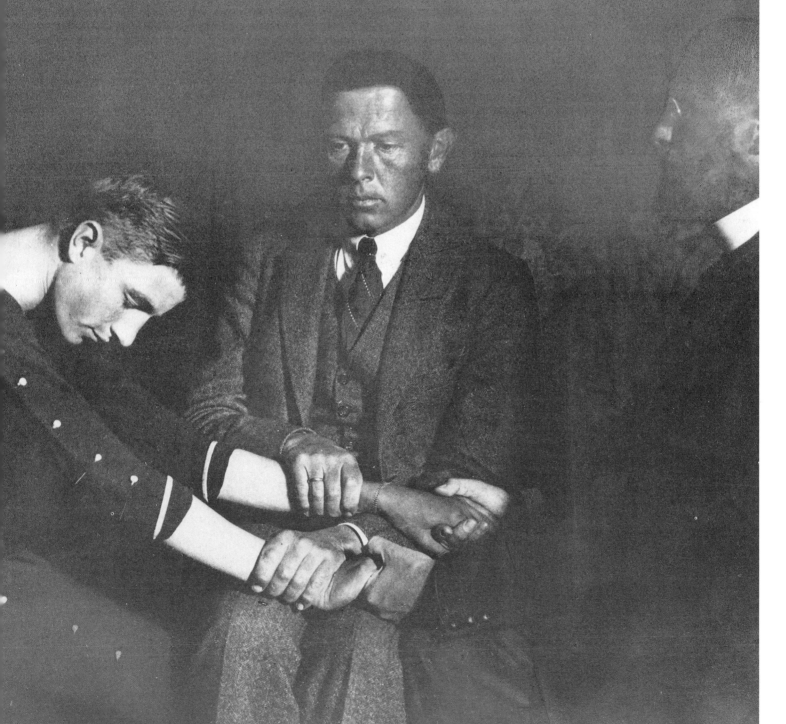

Josef Schneider, seen left with his wife and psychic sons, kept a detailed record of Rudi's seances in two thick exercise books. These became known as his 'ghost books'.

cars and aeroplanes – a preoccupation he shared with his brother Willi, five years his senior.

There are slight variations in the accounts of how their mediumistic activities began. The most widely told version is that in the early spring of 1919, officers stationed at Braunau began buying large quantities of paper from the print shop below the Schneiders' flat. The family discovered that the officers were holding spirit seances, and the paper was needed for recording spirit messages being spelt out by a *planchette* – a small board mounted on castors, and with a pencil attached.

Mrs Schneider and some friends decided to experiment with a *planchette* themselves, but without success. When some of the Schneider boys returned home one afternoon, they also tried but the *planchette* would not move. It was only when Willi arrived and took a turn that the *planchette* began to slide across the paper. Josef Schneider, who was affectionately known as *Vater* ('Father') Schneider, explained what happened:

'It began to write "Olga" in beautiful handwriting. Everyone was astonished and someone from the circle called out: "Well, what sort of an Olga are you then?" The reply was: "I was the mistress of the King of Bavaria, called Lola Montez." Now the questioning began and every day until midnight we did table turning and writing.'

Initially, the *planchette* appeared to move most fluently when Willi's hand was resting on it. Then, one day, it apparently moved when his hand was above it. As the questioning continued, Olga did not repeat or insist upon her claim that she was Lola Montez, a colourful and tempestuous Irish-Spanish dancer, created Countess von Landsfeld by King Ludwig I who had to abdicate his throne in 1848, some claim, because of his liaison with Lola.

Lola Montez, the dancer and famous beauty, right, had a notorious liaison with King Ludwig of Bavaria which may have cost him his throne. At first, Olga – Willi Schneider's spirit guide – claimed to be Lola; but Olga could not understand English even though Lola had been the daughter of a British army officer; nor could Olga give any details of Lola's life.

" THE FACT REMAINS THAT RUDI HAS BEEN SUBJECTED TO THE MOST MERCILESS TRIPLE CONTROL EVER IMPRESSED UPON A MEDIUM IN THIS OR ANY OTHER COUNTRY AND HAS COME THROUGH THE ORDEAL WITH FLYING COLOURS. THE GENUINENESS OF THE PHENOMENA... HAS IMPRESSED... SCIENTISTS, DOCTORS, BUSINESSMEN, PROFESSIONAL MAGICIANS, JOURNALISTS, ETC. *"*

HARRY PRICE

History tells how Lola could speak fluent English, whereas Olga could not even understand it. And, indeed, on later occasions, when Olga was asked to give details about Lola's life, she was unable to do so. It therefore seems likely that her identity was wished on her by the seance participants, but not by Willi.

Vater Schneider asked Olga if they could help her in any way. She wrote that they could indeed: would they have some masses said for the repose of her soul, please? The family were devout enough Catholics to comply with her request, though not sufficiently obedient members of their Church to desist from having seances. The masses were said, and seances continued. Olga was apparently grateful for their help and promised that, in return for their kindness, she would make their name famous throughout the world. It was a promise that she kept: the events that day signalled the beginning of a series of remarkable paranormal phenomena that were to startle the world.

Olga instructed the family to cover a kitchen stool with a large cloth and to place objects – including handkerchiefs and a basinful of water – near to it. Willi sat next to the stool and, within a short time, strange things started to happen. The water splashed out of the bowl, two tiny hands appeared to materialise from nowhere, the sound of clapping was heard, and objects placed near the

It was in the small Austrian city of Braunau, below, that Willi and Rudi Schneider were born and brought up.

Witnesses who saw the ectoplasm produced by Willi, below right, described it as a cobweb-like substance, or like an undulating, phosphorescent fog emanating from the boy's head.

stool were said to move. A handkerchief was also drawn beneath the cloth and then thrown out with knots tied in the four corners. Throughout the activities, Willi seemed unconcerned and to be enjoying the confusion that was being created around him.

KEEN OBSERVER

One of the witnesses was Captain Kogelnik, a man not naturally predisposed to believe in occult goings-on and rather inclined to dismiss them as antiquated, medieval rubbish. However, that first encounter with Willi Schneider's mediumship was to transform his outlook. According to Kogelnik, in those early days before Willi became an international celebrity, his ability to produce phenomena was at its height: 'Not even the slightest attempt was made by him to support the super-normal phenomena through normal means. He never fell into trance: he himself watched the manifestations with as much interest as any other person present.'

Kogelnik described how, on one occasion, the cloth over the stool lifted and a small hand emerged: 'I quickly and firmly grasped it and was just about to draw out from the table what I thought must be there – when I found my closed fist was empty and a heavy blow was dealt against it.'

As Kogelnik returned to the Schneider household and regularly witnessed Willi's skills, he became increasingly convinced that he was observing genuine physical phenomena. They were, he wrote, quite splendid:

'A zither was put on the floor, close to the tablecloth, and out from under the table there came a small hand with four fingers stroking the strings and trying to play. This hand was well visible, looked like that of a baby and was very well developed in every detail as far as the wrist, above which it passed off into a thin... glimmering ray which disappeared behind the tablecloth... A large brush was put before the tablecloth. The hand grasped it and began energetically to brush the floor in front of and behind the cloth... '

To begin with, Olga had written out her wishes and instructions while Willi was fully awake. After a time, however, she began to speak through him while he was in a trance. On these occasions, his voice came out as an unfamiliar hoarse whisper. Also at this stage, another odd phenomenon occurred: Willi began producing ectoplasm. Kogelnik described it as being a cobweb-like substance, first wrapped around the medium's face, but soon materialising on one shoulder, then the other. The substance seemed to disappear without a trace. One day, Olga invited Kogelnik to take a closer look. From a distance of about 10 inches (25 centimetres), he saw a faint, undulating phosphorescent fog being emitted from Willi's head. It eventually appeared to settle on Willi's hair and rested there like a cap, before being withdrawn into the body through his nose.

But this was not the most extraordinary occurrence. On one occasion, a phantom that stood 5 feet (1.5 metres) tall gracefully danced a tango for delighted onlookers before finally disappearing, perhaps in search of a partner, some of the witnesses ventured to suggest.

The flashlight picture, below, of one of Willi's sittings reveals a fake 'phantom' pinned to the curtain. But many people, including the novelist Thomas Mann, above, were convinced that Willi's powers were genuine.

*In*Focus

THE EYES HAD IT
Vater Schneider's ghost books, a complete record of Rudi's seances, were to help Rudi when an accusation of fraud was levelled against him. Two Viennese professors, Stefan Meyer and Karl Przibram, who had attended a seance with Rudi, later claimed that the controller had been influencing the sitting. Vater Schneider was able to defend his son's integrity by producing the very page, *right*, on which the two professors had endorsed the seance record, one of them adding for good measure the words '*Die Kontrolle war einwandfrei*' – 'the control was perfect'. They were therefore obliged to retract the claim that they had caught Rudi cheating, and instead had to content themselves with asserting that they had found a 'natural' way of producing such phenomena.

Not surprisingly, Willi's phenomena soon attracted local and then international attention. Various scientists went to Braunau in order to investigate. Among the most important figures in psychical research in Europe at that time was Baron von Schrenck-Nötzing. Kogelnik contacted him, aware that he would certainly be interested in Willi and the phenomena that he was producing.

SYSTEMATIC EXPERIMENTS
Schrenck-Nötzing began systematic experiments with the boy in December 1921. These were to continue for several years, and altogether he had 124 seances with Willi, publishing his findings in 1924. Twenty-seven university teachers and 29 other interested people, including doctors and writers, participated in these experiments, the results of which were claimed to be strongly positive. What is more, phenomena reported as happening in the Schneider household were said to have been repeated in the laboratory.

Among those who carried out investigations were Dr E.J. Dingwall and Harry Price who, together, visited Munich in May 1922. It was apparently with some amusement that Schrenck-Nötzing allowed the two Englishmen to search for trap doors and false walls. Having satisfied themselves that intruders could get in only through the front door, this was locked and sealed for the duration of the experiments. Unaffected by these conditions, Willi produced a number of extraordinary phenomena, including the levitation of a table, which rose with such force that Dingwall was unable to hold it down. After a series of tests, Dingwall thought the evidence strong enough to point to phenomena that were, indeed, the work of unexplained 'supernormal agencies'. At that point, he felt he could 'scarcely entertain with patience' the idea that all involved were engaged in a hoax. Unfortunately, however, Dingwall was not to maintain his conviction. Indeed, he suggested, some time later, that Schrenck-Nötzing must have somehow been

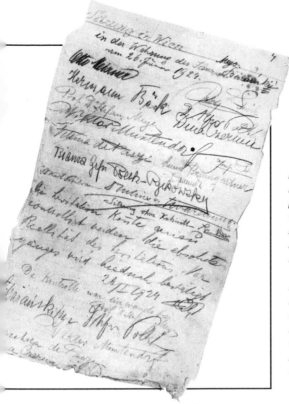

learned what was needed by way of documentation and evidence. His long experience with Willi had helped to convince him of the need to keep a systematic account of every seance. In the case of Rudi, this was a substantial number.

Every time there was a sitting, he entered the names of those present, the date and the place in an exercise book. Then he – or someone appointed to do so — gave an account of what had happened at the sitting. And, finally, all those participating were asked to sign the record alongside any comments they cared to make.

The two thick exercise books that Vater Schneider managed to fill make fascinating reading. They were always described as Vater Schneider's *Geisterbücher* – or ghost books. He refused to be parted from them in his lifetime.

These books are fading now; the binding is extremely frail, but the accounts of the sittings can still be read quite easily. Altogether they contain details of 269 sittings, from 8 December 1923 to 1 January 1932, and the painstakingly collected reports provide good evidence for the genuineness of Rudi Schneider's psychic powers.

responsible for what they had witnessed, though it is difficult to see how the Baron could have achieved such a feat.

Willi's mediumship gradually began to wane and, by the time he came to be investigated in London in 1924, the only phenomena he now seemed capable of producing were, to say the least, very disappointing. However, in 1919, before the decline had become firmly established, Olga made one of her strangest announcements. In the hoarse, hurried whisper that was characteristic of Willi in trance, she stated that she wanted to contact Rudi, and that he was in fact a stronger medium than Willi. The Schneider parents objected: Rudi was only 11 years old, he could not stay up late, and he would be frightened. Olga was adamant. 'He will come!' she said. And he did; for even as the Schneiders were arguing with Olga, the door opened and Rudi entered the room. He looked as if he were sleepwalking: his eyes were tightly closed and his hands outstretched. The moment he sat down, phenomena started to occur.

RISING STAR

Rudi now went into a trance and spoke as Olga. Willi, meanwhile, appeared to take on a new personality who announced herself as being 'Mina' and who spoke in a voice that was quite distinct from the one previously used by Willi when in trance. Olga was never again to speak through Willi and, with the phenomena he could produce already in decline, his younger brother Rudi now became very much the focus of attention.

Schrenck-Nötzing took an interest from the earliest days of Rudi's mediumship, and experiments were begun at once. At first, they were held in Braunau but, later, the boy was investigated at the Baron's own laboratory in Munich. The powers that Rudi seemed to possess were equal to those that his brother once had.

From the outset, Vater Schneider decided to keep a record of Rudi's progress, and quickly

Britain's Society for Psychical Research (SPR) was fortunate enough in its early days to be able to call upon the services of highly intelligent, well-educated sensitives with open minds – mostly women, incidentally, who according to prevailing custom, used their married names: Mrs Piper, Mrs Thompson, Mrs Leonard, Mrs Garrett, and a number of others.

Some of these women were 'physical' sensitives but most were 'mental' mediums – which may be significant, for physical mediums have become progressively rarer as methods of investigation have become more sophisticated. Cynics may leap to the conclusion that the likelihood of being caught as a fraud is so great these days that few dare to attempt to demonstrate 'physical' mediumship. But an alternative view is that the very act of setting up the elaborate apparatus necessary for investigation may inhibit the delicate, barely understood mechanism that produces the phenomenon. There also seems occasionally to be an 'experimenter effect', whereby sceptical and even merely objective experimenters may have a dampening effect on the activities of the seance room.

Although mediums, such as those listed above, produced very convincing results, members of the SPR were divided over the major question of proof of the afterlife. But they did agree that thought transference – including the communication of feelings, images, sounds, and even scents – had been proved beyond reasonable doubt. And although more than three decades were to pass before J. B. Rhine's work shifted the emphasis from psychical research (the scientific study of the paranormal) to parapsychology (treating psychic phenomena as expressions of little-understood mental activity), extra-sensory perception and psychokinesis were already being taken as alternative explanations for the mediums' purported 'proof' of survival.

It has been suggested that ESP can explain the often uncannily accurate information that a medium gives a sitter. For, through ESP, the human mind may 'pick the brains' of others, without being conscious of doing so, and mistakenly believe the information is coming from a dead relative. *PK* – psychokinesis or 'mind over matter' – meanwhile, is the mysterious force exerted by the mind over inanimate objects. This would explain the so-called 'spirit' table-turnings and rappings of the seance room in terms of a natural, if rare, function of the human mind. Some minds are even thought capable of gleaning information (through a facility known as

A soul being ferried across the river of death – the Styx – is depicted above, in the 16th-century painting by Joachim Patinir. It reveals a blend of Classical and Christian beliefs: the Styx and its ferryman, Charon, were believed by the ancient Greeks to carry the dead to their appointed place for eternity. The dead were buried with coins in their mouths so that they could pay the ferryman. Failure to pay resulted in damnation. The Christian concepts of purgatory, paradise and hell are also shown in this painting on either side of the dreaded river.

AFTERLIFE

Pluto, ruler of Hades, or the realm of the underworld believed by the Greeks to be a real geographical location that dead souls reached through caves, is seen left on a Greek vase, together with Persephone, whom Pluto made queen. Hades was said to be a shadowy and sinister abode, but not a place of active judgement or punishment. However, at a popular level, there was a widespread suspicion that Hades was much more fearsome territory.

GESP or general extra-sensory perception) from any written, printed or other kind of record (including presumably, microfilm), arranging and producing it as a coherent account. Such a concept, if true, destroys any chance of proving survival as a fact, for any message from a deceased person – no matter how accurate or how personal the information given – could theoretically be the result of this facility. Such stores of the sum of human knowledge are known by Theosophists as the 'Akashic records'; and certain sensitive people have long been believed to have access to its 'files'. So it could be that, in some unknown way, the 'cross-referencing' necessary for a medium to produce a convincing story of someone's life on Earth has already been done.

There are two other major arguments sometimes presented against evidence for survival as provided by mediums. The first is that a sensitive's so-called 'control' or 'spirit guide' may be no more than an example of dissociated or multiple personality. This condition seems to be formed by the splitting-off of certain mental processes from the mainstream of consciousness. If these 'other selves' come to the surface, they have been known to take over completely, the condition becoming a serious illness. (There have even been cases where over a dozen completely distinct personalities have inhabited the same body, either taking over in turns or fighting among themselves for possession.) Such manifestations have sometimes happened unexpectedly when apparently 'normal' people have been hypnotised. So perhaps a sensitive, by his or her very nature, may be more susceptible to the development of secondary personalities than the more down-to-earth or openly sceptical.

THE VERSATILE FORGER

There is also another extraordinary power of the human mind, known as *mythopoeia*, involving an ability to create myths or detailed stories that are strikingly convincing and that frequently surface during hypnotic regression as 'past lives'. The result may be 'subconscious forgery', enabling some sensitives to imitate the voices, mannerisms, handwriting and even the style of musical composition or drawing of the (sometimes famous) dead. All this may also be at second hand, drawn from the minds of others. *Mythopoeia* may also be responsible for the ability of people in trances to sing or pour out a flood of unintelligible language, known as 'speaking in tongues'. It is a theory that provides an alternative explanation for the many bizarre phenomena that have been taken as 'proof' of survival.

The deaths of the SPR's founder members, notably that of F.W.H. Myers in 1901, were followed by a new phenomenon, that of the 'cross-correspondences'. These were fragmentary messages received at different times and places through two or more sensitives, unconnected with each other. The messages, often apparently nonsensical when taken separately, made perfect sense when fitted together. The compiling of the cross-correspondences took over 30 years. The timing of their beginning, coinciding as it did with the deaths of those whose main preoccupation in life had been to understand the mysteries of death, seems to many investigators to prove beyond doubt who was behind the experiment. Indeed, it seemed

as if the founders of the SPR had arranged a meeting beyond the grave and said: 'Any normal message we send will be ascribed to thought transference. Let us devise a method of communication that will not be open to such an interpretation.'

PAINSTAKING EXPERIMENT

Certainly, no messages easily ascribable to thought transference had ever been communicated in fragments to different mediums before. And the subject matter of the messages – poetry and erudite classical allusions – was highly characteristic of the group of deceased SPR members. Although, to a certain extent, *GESP* could account for much of the material of the cross-correspondences, many researchers believe that they are the best evidence yet of survival. Even so, all they do is attempt to convince us, in as many ingenious ways as possible, of the continued existence of certain individuals. (The dead Myers is alleged to have found the effort of communication trying. To him, 'endlessly presenting my credentials' proved frustrating in the extreme.) But even assuming its authenticity, this massive, painstaking experiment tells us little of what happens when we die, except that we retain something of our earthly habits of thought and some traits of personality.

Some seances have occasionally been interrupted by 'drop-in' spirits, who are unknown to anyone

> **THERE ARE MANY DIFFERENT REGIONS IN THIS AFTERWORLD... THE INDIVIDUAL AFTER DEATH TENDS TO GRAVITATE INTO REGIONS WHERE HE ASSOCIATES WITH PEOPLE WHO ARE LIKE HIMSELF. HERE HIS ENVIRONMENT IS CREATED JOINTLY OUT OF THE COLLECTIVE MEMORIES, ATTITUDES, AND DESIRES OF THOSE WHO ARE SPIRITUALLY IN TUNE WITH HIM.**
>
> **ALSON J. SMITH, IMMORTALITY: THE SCIENTIFIC EVIDENCE**

The ancient Egyptians believed the afterlife to be very similar to that on Earth but more pleasurable, as shown above left, in a depiction of idealised farming in the world beyond.

Model slaves, such as those above, were believed to assume real duties in the afterlife in the service of the master in whose tomb they were put.

present, and yet provide information about themselves that is later discovered to be substantially correct. Again, this phenomenon could perhaps be explained by *GESP*. But why should a sensitive pick up information about someone in whom no one present has any interest?

Witnesses of the dying often report that dead friends and relatives are apparently seen by them just before death – coming to welcome the newly deceased to the 'other side'. Such experiences may well be hallucinations, a mechanism of nature to ease the passing from life. But this does not, of course, explain those cases where the dying have exclaimed at the 'visit' of a relative whose own death was unknown to them.

An early 15th-century view of heaven as a peaceful garden is shown right. *In days when life was short (and youth and beauty, tragically brief), an eternal period of relaxation in beautiful surroundings had an obvious emotive appeal. Here, the garden of heaven is shown peopled with young, healthy and attractive souls. They relax in each other's company – reading, picking choice fruits, playing musical instruments and holding pleasant conversations. They are also all dressed in the finest and most fashionable clothes. The wall suggests the exclusivity of heaven and a sense of security after the trials of life.*

Since the 1960s, research has been carried out into the experiences of people who have clinically 'died' – often on the operating table – and who have come back to life. They nearly all report similar experiences, whether they had previously believed in survival or not. They report being conscious of leaving their bodies and passing through a dark tunnel with a light at the end. When they emerged from the tunnel, they were met by a radiant figure, often too bright to be seen clearly. This being, however, is identified differently, according to the individual's religious 'vocabulary'; for the westerner, for instance, he is usually taken to be Christ. They may also be aware of the presence of dead friends or relatives, and are filled with tremendous peace and joy. Yet they are told that their 'time' has not yet come and that they have to return. With the greatest unwillingness, they then re-enter their body. Significantly, people who have had this sort of experience are never afraid of death.

Another mass of evidence that we exist apart from our physical forms concerns out-of-the-body experiences, also referred to as *OOBEs*. Many

The medieval concept of hell was a place of brutal torment, believed to be both physical and spiritual. Although sophisticated theologians of the day argued that the real anguish of hell was the knowledge that one was eternally denied the presence of God, most ordinary people believed that hell was the proverbial fiery pit, as illustrated above.

people have had the curious experience of finding themselves hovering over their sleeping – or unconscious – bodies: this most often happens in moments of crisis, during accidents, torture, or while undergoing an operation. Some people later astonish surgeons and nurses by telling them exactly what they had done and said while carrying out the operation. A few even claim to be able to leave their bodies at will: and this, to them, is proof that they exist in a non-physical dimension and that this aspect of them will survive bodily death.

In some instances, tests have been arranged by the living so that, after their deaths, they might prove their continued existence by revealing,

*"*THERE WILL ALWAYS BE PEOPLE WHO REMAIN SEEMINGLY UNTOUCHED BY A DISPLAY OF SPIRIT POWER . . . THE SCEPTIC WHO REFUTES THE FACT OF ANOTHER EXISTENCE BEYOND DEATH AND LEAVES A DEMONSTRATION WITH NOTHING BUT SCORN FOR MEDIUMSHIP MAY BE THE PERSON HOLDING THE GREATEST FEAR OF DYING.*"*

STEPHEN O'BRIEN,

VISIONS OF ANOTHER WORLD

through mediums, the solutions to puzzles. So far, none of these has been notably successful, though the number of tests arranged may be too small to be significant. Lovers or friends have also made pacts that the one dying first should appear to the other, under certain specific circumstances. Allegedly, they have done so. But grief frequently produces hallucinations of the deceased: indeed, they seem to be part of the natural mourning process, acting as a comfort.

Supposed evidence for reincarnation, meanwhile, sets out not only to show that we survive and are reborn (perhaps many times), but also to offer clues as to why we are born at all. Hypnotic regression into 'past lives'; some children's spontaneous memories of being someone else; the 'far memory' of some adults; some *déjà vu* experiences; all these, though subject to other explanations, point to reincarnation as a distinct possibility. Many people even believe that we must submit to a string of different earthly lives until we achieve near perfection of soul: then we become 'gods' or progress on a purely spiritual plane.

Dr Ian Stevenson, of the University of Virginia in the United States, has made a detailed and scholarly investigation into evidence for reincarnation. He has amassed hundreds of cases of alleged 'past lives', reaching the conclusion that 'a rational man . . . can believe in reincarnation on the basis of evidence'. However, for the majority of people, such a belief will remain a matter of faith alone.

The Buddah, above left, suggests calm and enlightenment. The ancient Chinese painting, above right, meanwhile, depicts the Buddhist 'seventh hell', where the souls of the condemned are said to be chased by ferocious dogs and devils into a deadly river.

Since the 1960s, tape recorders have allegedly been picking up voices of the dead. This phenomenon has since become something of a cult. However, all that can be said of it so far is that, whatever the source of the voices, they do not add to our information about the afterlife.

Despite fast-growing interest in all aspects of the paranormal and psychical research, it is true to say that the majority of believers in survival of the spirit follow some sort of religion; and for them, a belief in the afterlife is entirely a matter of faith. Such faith goes back a very long way; and the oldest known burial customs show that ancient Man believed in survival.

The world's more sophisticated religions, however, differ widely in their concept of Man's ultimate goal. Hindus and Buddhists teach that we finally escape from the miseries of earthly incarnations into a mystical and blissful unity with Brahma, the Supreme Principle, or enter Nirvana, in which the self is lost in the infinite.

In the ancient world, Greeks, Romans and Hebrews believed that the spirit departed to an unsatisfactory existence in a shadowy Hades or *Sheol*. Later, Jews accepted the concept of the resurrection of the righteous to companionship with the Patriarchs; but even today, Judaism does not teach a doctrine of eternal life for everyone.

Believer or atheist, philosopher or materialist, each one of us must die. Only then will we find out the truth for certain.

SURVIVAL – THE SOLID EVIDENCE?

PERHAPS THE MOST CONTROVERSIAL AREA OF PSYCHICAL RESEARCH IS THAT OF PHYSICAL MEDIUMSHIP. HOW GENUINE MIGHT IT BE?

Author and debunker William Marriott is seen below, surrounded by a fake medium's materialisation props. In normal lighting – and without benefit of the heightened atmosphere of the seance room – such sheeted masks look laughably crude. Yet these very fabrications fooled a great many witnesses.

One of the ironies of the paranormal is that often the best evidence offered for the existence of a spiritual realm is actually produced in a physical form. To some, it may seem absurd that raps, moving tables and levitating trumpets are manifestations produced by spirits; but explaining such phenomena in other ways is, perhaps, no more persuasive.

Such physical phenomena do not occur in isolation: a human catalyst almost always seems to be responsible. The birth of Spiritualism in Hydesville, in the United States, in 1848, actually came about through simple raps that apparently formed the basis of communication between a dead pedlar and the Fox family. Within a few years, the three Fox sisters – Kate, Margaretta and Leah – became world-famous as mediums, and many others discovered that, under the right conditions, they could produce physical phenomena, too.

SPIRIT MACHINE

Elsewhere in the United States, during the early 1850s, farmer Jonathan Koons began conducting his own experiments with physical mediumship. He claimed that the spirits had told him he was 'the most powerful medium on earth'. Following their instructions, he built a small log cabin alongside his farmhouse in Ohio, so that he and his eight children – all of whom were said to be psychic – could hold seances. It was equipped with musical instruments and other items with which the spirits could play. In appearance, it was like a tiny theatre, with seats for up to 30. When the audience was settled, Koons would turn out the lights and play hymns on his fiddle until unseen hands would lift other musical instruments and join in. During such noisy concerts, a tambourine would circle above the heads of the audience, trumpets floated in the air and voices spoke. Spirit hands held phosphor-coated paper to illuminate some of the manifestations. Koons even built a 'spirit machine' – a complex piece of zinc and copper apparatus that the spirits said would help collect and focus the magnetic aura used for their physical demonstrations. According to Koons, when this device was in service, the spirits could triumph over the laws of gravity and cohesion, enabling them to move heavy objects at speed and play instruments.

Just 3 miles (5 kilometres) away, and without the help of a 'spirit machine', John Tipple and his children gave very similar performances in his 'spirit house', which was also said to have been built under instructions from the next world.

Jonathan Koons never charged for the seances he held and there is no evidence of fraud. But, despite Spiritualism's general popularity at that time, he encountered open hostility, particularly from his neighbours. His home was attacked by

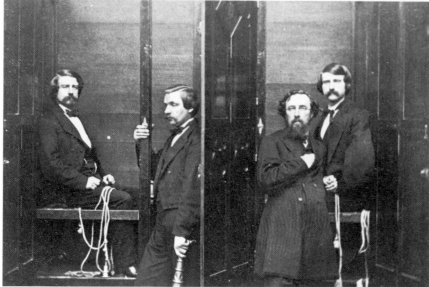

mobs, his children were beaten, and his barns and fields were set alight, forcing him to leave the area. He and his family eventually became Spiritualist missionaries.

Another American family with a similar, eventful seance room were the Davenports. Physical phenomena in the form of raps and strange noises were said to have been heard in their Buffalo, New York, home in 1846, two years before the Hydesville episodes. At that time, Ira Davenport was seven years old and his brother William was five. Four years later, the two boys and their sister Elisabeth began table-turning with impressive results. The table moved, raps were heard and a spirit was said to have controlled Ira's hand and to have written messages. The three children are also reported to have levitated simultaneously at least once. On the

The Davenport brothers were two of the most famous mediums of the late 19th century, exciting both extreme adulation and bitter hostility. Their stage show featured what was, in effect, a portable seance room – a three-doored cabinet, as shown top. When Harry Houdini met Ira Davenport, in the early 1900s, above, he claimed that Davenport confessed to the fact that he and his brother were never anything but conjurers and that they had taught the famous magician Harry Kellar, left, many of his tricks.

fifth night of their experiments, Ira was told by the raps to take a pistol and shoot at a corner of the room. He did so; and at the moment it fired, they saw another phantom figure holding the pistol. It then vanished and the gun fell to the floor.

According to the Davenport children, they were told by the spirits to allow investigators to tie them up in ropes to prove that they were not producing the noises and other manifestations that occurred in their darkened room. This they did to the satisfaction of many visitors, including sceptics.

The Davenports' mediumship was no more remarkable than that of other physical mediums in the mid to late 1800s, but what set them apart was their decision to demonstrate their powers in public. In order to do this, the Davenport brothers constructed a three-door cabinet that was, in effect, a portable seance room. Members of the audience were invited to tie them up securely. But as soon as the doors were closed, strange phenomena occurred. Raps and bangs were heard, hands waved through a small window in the cabinet's centre door, and musical instruments were played. A member of the audience was often invited to sit inside the darkened cabinet while these manifestations were being produced – yet at the end of the demonstrations, the brothers were always still found to be securely tied.

Ethel Beenham, secretary to psychical researcher Harry Price, *left, demonstrates the relative ease with which a large piece of cheesecloth can be held in the mouth – a common method of producing fake ectoplasm.*

The Polish medium Stanislawa Tomczyk, below, *could levitate a table simply by lifting up her hands. Extensively investigated by the eminent European psychical researcher Dr Julien Ochorowicz, she was discovered to have extremely impressive psychokinetic powers – although some sceptics have suggested that the objects she moved, apparently through PK, were attached to her hands by fine string. There seem to be no grounds for this allegation, however.*

untied and the professor had the rope twisted around his neck. But even so, the newspaper did not award its $500 prize to the Davenports.

The controversy over the boys from Buffalo came to a head when they took their show on the road in Europe where they encountered hostile audiences. Their reception in London and other English cities was particularly sour and things became difficult in Liverpool where two members of the inspection committee, selected by the audience, secured Ira and William with a complicated knot. The brothers claimed that it was restricting their circulation – but a doctor who examined them disagreed. The problem was resolved by a helper who used a knife to cut the knot. A riot broke out on the following night, and the Davenports left Liverpool in haste. Elsewhere in Britain, they received threats that made them decide to end their tour prematurely. As they wrote at the time:

'Were we mere jugglers, we should meet with no violence, or we should find protection. Could we declare that these things done in our presence were deception of the senses, we should no doubt reap a plentiful harvest of money and applause... But we are not jugglers, and truthfully declare that we are not, and we are mobbed from town to town, our property destroyed and our lives imperilled.'

Harry Houdini, the famous escapologist and illusionist, tells a different story. He befriended Ira in the early 1900s, and claimed that Ira admitted that they were no more than conjurers. There is no evidence to support that charge; but it is a fact that Harry Kellar, who was also an internationally famous magician, was employed by the Davenports at one time and, in Houdini's words, 'afterwards learned to do tricks which altogether surpassed their efforts in rope-tying and escape.'

It is impossible to know now, over a century later, if the Davenports were genuine or fraudulent,

It was an impressive and entertaining display, and large audiences flocked to the best theatres in town when the Davenport brothers took their 'public cabinet seance' on tour in America. But it created the same sort of controversy between believers and sceptics as Uri Geller was to bring about in the early 1970s. Certainly, any competent escapologist could get in and out of tied ropes in the way the Davenports did, but that does not necessarily make them frauds. They never claimed to be Spiritualists, but they did maintain that their powers were paranormal – which was why, when the *Boston Courier* offered a $500 prize for the production of genuine physical phenomena, the Davenports applied.

A committee of professors from Harvard University tested them on behalf of the newspaper. Ira and William were tied up, and the ropes passed through holes bored in the cabinet and knotted on the outside. One of the committee members, Professor Benjamin Pierce, then climbed into the cabinet and the doors were closed.

What happened next is a little uncertain. We know that the *Boston Courier* denied one version of the event, which was written by T.L. Nichols, the Davenports' biographer – this was apparently fairly favourable. But Professor Pierce would neither confirm nor deny it. What is certain is that, when the cabinet doors were opened, the brothers were

and the theatricality that surrounded their seances must have made it just as difficult for eyewitnesses to decide. But experiments with physical mediums under carefully controlled conditions have occasionally provided very strong evidence in favour of the genuineness of the manifestations they produce. Sir William Crookes was one of the first physicists to explore the psychic force responsible for producing raps and movements. He tested the most famous of all physical mediums, Daniel Dunglas Home, and became convinced that he possessed strong psychic powers.

Another early investigator of physical forces was Marc Thury, professor of physics and natural history at the University of Geneva, Switzerland, who witnessed the simultaneous levitation of two pianos in the presence of an 11-year-old boy, in the 1850s. Professor Thury suggested that the human body was able to exude a substance that was then manipulated by an unseen force to produce such startling effects. This was the forerunner of the

Kate Goligher, an Irish medium of the 1920s, is seen below, apparently levitating a table with the aid of ectoplasmic rods. These seem to be obviously fake, especially when seen in close-up, opposite, centre; yet Goligher was never proved to be fraudulent.

ectoplasmic theory, and one that gained ground with many investigators whose observations appeared to provide a degree of confirmation.

LOOK – NO HANDS!

What is puzzling in such cases as the levitating pianos is that, even if the boy had the opportunity to cheat, there is no way in which he could have lifted two such heavy items – or even one of them for that matter. Dr d'Oliveira Feijao, professor of surgery at Lisbon University in Portugal, made a similar observation in the presence of a non-professional medium, Countess Castelwitch, who discovered her powers in 1913. The doctor testified that at her seances: 'Blows were struck, the loudest being on the glass of the bookcase. Articles of furniture sometimes moved. Heavy chairs moved about the room . . . large and heavy books were flung on the floor (our hands being linked all the time).'

At one of the countess' seances, a table, weighing 160 pounds (73 kilograms), was raised on two legs when she touched it lightly. Another smaller table that was strengthened with sheet-iron was torn into 200 pieces by invisible hands, which then piled the pieces into a corner of the room.

A few years earlier, Dr Julien Ochorowicz, an eminent European psychical researcher, had carried out experiments with a young Polish girl, Stanislawa Tomczyk, who was reported to have the ability to move objects without touching them, to stop the hands of a clock and even influence a roulette wheel when she chose the numbers. Dr Ochorowicz not only witnessed the levitation of small objects between Stanislawa Tomczyk's fingers, he also managed to capture the phenomenon on photographs. Sceptics, however, suggested that he had been fooled and that the medium was suspending the items with very thin thread. The researcher replied that, during these demonstrations, he had passed his hand between the object and the medium's fingers and the levitation was maintained. He put forward the theory that she was able to produce 'rigid rays' from her hands to cause these paranormal effects. Stanislawa Tomczyk never gave seances professionally. She confined the displays to scientific experiments and married Everard Feilding, one of the Society for Psychical Research's leading and most sceptical investigators.

Another physical medium who allowed her powers to be studied in the laboratory was Anna Rasmussen, a Danish woman who discovered her startling powers at the age of 12. A number of scientists conducted experiments with her in the 1920s, including Professor Christian Winther of the Polytechnic Academy of Copenhagen.

The professor held 116 seances with her in 1928, at each one of which some form of physical phenomenon was produced. The medium remained conscious throughout and usually sat talking, reading or taking refreshments, apparently unconcerned and detached from the manifestations that repeatedly occurred in her presence. These included the production of raps – apparently emanating from her left shoulder – which would answer questions. What impressed the scientists most, however, was the degree of control she could exert over the phenomena. In full daylight, she was able to cause the movement of pendulums suspended in a sealed

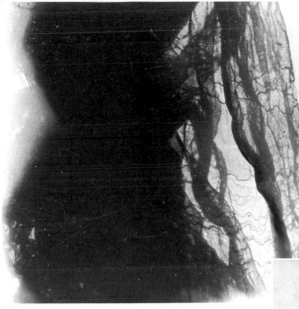

The dark, lace-like ectoplasm, above left, was produced at one of the Goligher seances in Belfast in the 1920s. Almost all such samples are said to have dematerialised, and only one specimen remains in the possession of the Society for Psychical Research – but it is indisputably cheesecloth.

glass case at a distance from her. She was even able to move one pendulum at a time, leaving the others undisturbed, and to make it move in whatever direction was requested.

FRAUD-PROOF EXPERIMENTS?

Nearly 30 years later, the same medium – then Anna Rasmussen Melloni – was asked by psychical researchers if she could repeat the demonstration for them. Several successful experiments were carried out in 1956; but because her own pendulums were used to produce the most impressive results, this detracted from her achievement in the opinion of some experimenters.

While the early tests with Anna Rasmussen were being conducted in Denmark, a British medium was giving the last seances of her brief but spectacular (and strictly nonprofessional) career. Stella Cranshaw, a young nurse, had been discovered by the colourful and controversial psychical researcher Harry Price in the early 1920s. She agreed to be tested at his National Laboratory of Psychical Research in London and he devised elaborate, ingenious equipment, including a supposedly fraud-proof seance table, to test her powers, as well as imposing stringent controls.

This table was really two – one inside another. The top of the inner table was fitted with a hinged trap door that could be opened only from the underside. Musical instruments, such as a harmonica or bell, were placed on a shelf between the legs of the inner table, and a length of gauze was wrapped around the legs. The sides of each table were also enclosed in wooden trellises. These precautions made it impossible for anyone to be able to touch the objects on the inner shelf.

Stella Cranshaw sat at this table with other sitters, two of whom held her hands and feet throughout the proceedings. Soon after she had gone into a trance, sounds – such as the ringing of a bell or the playing of a harmonica – were heard coming from within the table. The trap door in the table top was pushed up from inside and, when a handkerchief was placed over it, sitters felt finger-like forms moving beneath it.

Stella Cranshaw, below left, a young British nurse, was discovered to be a powerful medium in the 1920s. Despite her undoubted gifts, she was never really interested in mediumship and never gave public seances.

The greatest achievement of Stella Cranshaw's mediumship, in Harry Price's eyes, was the successful manipulation of a telekinetiscope – a sensitive piece of apparatus that he had designed himself. It consisted of a small red light bulb, a battery and a telegraph key. When the key was pressed, the light would come on. To prevent this happening by normal means, Price designed the apparatus so that a soap bubble covered the key. During the course of a seance in the presence of Stella Cranshaw, the device would be placed inside a glass shade to prevent the soap bubble from drying out. The light would then be turned on, apparently by psychokinesis; and when the device was inspected later, the soap bubble was always found to be still intact.

Stella Cranshaw was tested over five years, but in spite of the remarkable phenomena witnessed during such demonstrations, she had little interest or enthusiasm for psychic work; and when she married in 1928, she stopped giving seances altogether. Other mediums, however, have continued to produce what seems to be tangible evidence of their strange abilities.

ONE OF THE BEST-DOCUMENTED CASES OF A MEDIUM PRODUCING ECTOPLASMIC FORMS IS THAT OF EVA C, MANY OF WHOSE MATERIALISATIONS WERE PHOTOGRAPHED

During the first decade of this century, a young French girl living in Algiers began to exhibit remarkable psychic powers. Marthe Béraud, the daughter of a French army officer, was apparently able to produce full-form materialisations of an ectoplasmic substance during seances. As her abilities as a medium became known, she came under the scrutiny of some of Europe's leading psychical researchers, many of whom were convinced

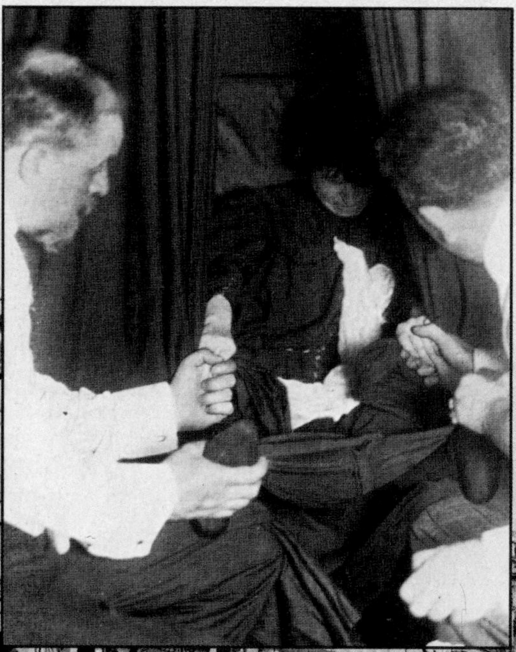

Eva C was born in around 1890 and grew up in Algiers, below, where she became engaged to the son of General Noel, at whose house seances were held, and where her powers as a medium were discovered. Unhappily, Eva's fiancé died before they could be married, but her career as a medium flourished. At seances in Paris, like the one held on 7 June 1911, left, Eva was able to produce ectoplasmic materialisations, even though her hands and feet were held by two witnesses throughout the proceedings.

that the phenomena produced by 'Eva C' – the pseudonym of Marthe Beraud – were genuine ectoplasmic 'teleplasms'.

But suspicion of fraud arose very early in Eva's career. In 1904, a lawyer name Marsault attended seances held at the Villa Carmen, home of the Noel family who ran a Spiritualist circle, and claimed that the young medium had confessed that she faked the phenomena for fun. Yet less than a year later, one of the most respected investigators of the day, Professor Charles Richet, published a favourable report of Eva's mediumship.

Richet elaborated upon his experience with Eva in his book *Thirty Years of Psychical Research*, and said he had been able to:

'See the first lineaments of materialisations as they were formed. A kind of liquid or pasty jelly emerges from the mouth or the breast of Marthe, which organises itself by degrees, acquiring the shape of a face or a limb... I have seen this paste spread on my knee, and slowly take form so as to show the rudiment of the radius, the cubitus, or metacarpal bone...'

Richet (who was professor of physiology at the Faculty of Medicine in Paris) admitted that these formations were often very imperfect. Sometimes

SHAPES FROM THE SHADOWS

they looked like flat images 'so that in spite of one-self, one is inclined to imagine some fraud, since what appears seems to be the materialisation of a semblance, and not of a being.'

But at other times, Eva did produce recognisable spirit forms. Richet witnessed one such materialisation at the Villa Carmen:

'At first, it was only a white, opaque spot, like a handkerchief, lying on the ground before the curtain, then this handkerchief quickly assumed the form of a human head level with the floor, and a few moments later it rose up in a straight line and became a small man enveloped in a kind of white burnous, who took two or three halting steps in front of the curtain and then sank to the floor and disappeared as if through a trap-door. But there was no trap-door.'

BEARDED SPIRIT

A spirit who regularly appeared at Eva's seances was Bien Boa, said to have died 300 years previously. One remarkable picture shows him with a thick beard, wearing a helmet, and draped with ectoplasm. Richet maintained that, on five or six occasions, he saw both Bien Boa and Eva at the same time. The phantom's eyes moved, and so did his lips as he tried to speak. The witnesses could also hear him breathing, and the professor used a flask containing a chemical solution to test if Bien Boa's breath contained carbon dioxide: it did.

At another seance, a beautiful Egyptian princess was seen. This spirit, said Richet, was well-defined and wore a gilt ribbon or diadem in her fair hair. She was laughing, and he could see her pearly teeth. Richet was told to bring scissors the following day so that he could cut a lock of the spirit's hair. When the woman materialised again, he saw that she had very abundant hair, though he had trouble distinguishing her face. Richet reported:

WITH SOME MEDIUMS, A KIND OF LIQUID OR PASTY JELLY EMERGES FROM THE MOUTH, FOREHEAD OR BREAST; WITH OTHERS, THIN, NARROW STALKS WHICH THICKEN... INTO MUSLIN-LIKE CURTAINS OR EVEN SOLID-SEEMING LIMBS AND BODIES ARE EXTRUDED.

CYRIL PERMUTT, PHOTOGRAPHING THE SPIRIT WORLD

Eva's manifestations were carefully investigated by such eminent psychical researchers as Baron von Schrenck-Nötzing and Professor Charles Richet, top, and Mme Juliette Bisson, shown above in her seance room.

At a seance held in Paris on 13 March 1911 with Schrenck-Nötzing, Richet and Mme Bisson in attendance, Eva produced ectoplasm that assumed the shape of hands, left.

'As I was about to cut a lock high up, a firm hand behind the curtain lowered mine, so that I cut only about six inches [15 centimetres] from the end... I have kept this lock: it is very fine, silky and undyed. Microscopical examination shows it to be real hair... Marthe's hair is very dark and she wears her hair very short.'

Was it perhaps possible that Eva was producing these phenomena by smuggling props into the seance room? Many other mediums have been caught doing so before and since, but Richet and other investigators went to great lengths to satisfy themselves that the medium was not using trickery.

At seances conducted by the German physician Baron von Schrenck-Nötzing over a four-year period, the most stringent precautions were taken. The seance cabinet, which was usually a curtained section of the room, was searched; and Eva was stripped naked in front of witnesses and then clothed in a close-fitting garment from neck to feet. Often her head was completely covered by a veil of tulle, which was then sewn to the other garment.

Despite all these measures, sceptics still suggested that Eva was somehow able to secrete props about her person. The investigators carried out mouth, vaginal and anal examinations, but the medium was never found to be hiding anything. Another theory was that she was able to swallow

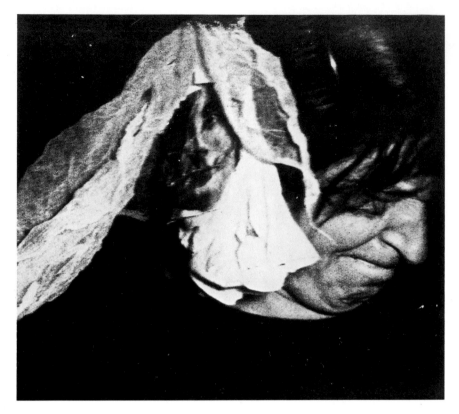

the props and regurgitate them during a seance. She was therefore given syrup of bilberries to drink, so that it would colour anything she had swallowed. But the ectoplasm that subsequently appeared was as white as before. On one occasion, Eva was even given an emetic before a seance, to make sure she had not swallowed muslin or paper. Within 10 minutes, she had vomited, and another theory was disproved. Even if she had managed to smuggle props into the seance room, the controls were so strict that it would seem to have been impossible for her to use them.

Throughout Schrenck-Nötzing's investigations, not a single seance was held in total darkness. A red light was used: at first this was a single lamp; but later on, the phenomena were witnessed beneath a six-lamp chandelier of more than 100 watts. The medium sat behind a curtain, or curtains, to provide her with the darkness necessary to produce ectoplasm. But she usually sat with her hands visible, drawing the curtains apart when phenomena occurred. At other times, witnesses held her hands all the time.

DAMAGING EVIDENCE

One of the investigators who conducted the seances with Schrenck-Nötzing was Juliette Bisson, in whose house Eva C lived for several years. To record their visual observations, the two researchers used a number of cameras (sometimes as many as nine), including stereoscopic equipment. These were arranged to take pictures simultaneously in order to record phenomena from a number of vantage points (including above and behind the curtain), not usually accessible to investigators. It was this arrangement that produced one of the most damaging pieces of evidence against Eva C. At a seance held in Paris on 27 November 1912, at which Schrenck-Nötzing and Mme Bisson

Eva is seen, above, producing ectoplasm in the form of a human face at a session in Paris on 22 November 1911. Although sceptics said that Eva's materialisations were unconvincing, others – such as Dr Gustave Geley – were sure that they were genuine. Geley described in detail how her ectoplasms were produced. Eva was first seated in a dark cabinet, and then entered a hypnotic state. When the phenomena started to appear, they produced painful sensations in her. She would sigh and moan, her groaning only ceasing when the forms were complete.

were the only observers, photographs were taken that showed the side view of a flat, creased disc, on which the words 'Le' in small type and 'Miro' in large type were visible. Schrenck-Nötzing commented: 'That is evidently meant to be "Le Miroir". We can just recognise the top of an "I" following the "O", but the next "R" is covered. I cannot form any opinion on this curious result.'

Others could, however, and were quick to suggest that the medium had used an image cut from the magazine *Le Miroir*. Yet Eva C's hands were in full view during the production of this ectoplasmic shape, according to Schrenck-Nötzing.

Schrenck-Nötzing published the picture, together with some candid criticisms, in 1914 in his book on the *Phenomena of Materialisation*, in which the pseudonym 'Eva C' was used for the first time. Perhaps Schrenck-Nötzing concealed the identity of the medium because he was afraid that an earlier allegation of fraud against her (in Algiers, when she was supposed to have confessed to cheating) would discredit his work.

This allegation had been made by an Arab coachman who had been dismissed by General Noel (in whose home the earlier seances took place) for theft. The coachman, who was called Areski, said he had 'played ghost' at the seances; he was even put on show dressed in white by a doctor in Algiers who wanted to expose the medium. But Areski's allegation is barely credible. He claimed that he entered the seance room with everyone else; and that, while the other sitters were examining the furniture, he would slip behind the curtain in readiness to play the part of a phantom. Richet, who attended these seances, dismissed the claim indignantly: 'Now, I declare formally and solemnly that during the seances – 20 in number – Areski was not once permitted to enter the seance room.'

KEEPING WATCH

Another allegation of fraud came from an observer who believed that Mme Bisson was collaborating with the medium, in order to dupe Schrenck-Nötzing. This doubting Thomas employed a Paris detective agency to keep watch on the two women, gather information and even acquire copies of Schrenck-Nötzing's seance photographs. But in the course of an eight-month enquiry, the agency failed to find any evidence of fraud, nor did it discover what material was being used to produce the materialisations.

The photographs themselves, many of which were published in Schrenck-Nötzing's book, would not convince anyone of the reality of materialisation. They appear to be crude fakes. Many show crumpled and creased two-dimensional images that seem to be attached to the medium's hair. They are a far cry from the fully-formed spirits that are said to walk and talk at the materialisation seances of the most powerful mediums.

Nevertheless, much of what occurred in the presence of Eva C is difficult to explain in normal terms, considering the strict controls imposed on her. At those seances that produced results (on average half the sittings were negative), it was a white substance that often appeared. This would change shape, move around slowly and throw out antennae-like spikes. Sometimes it would form

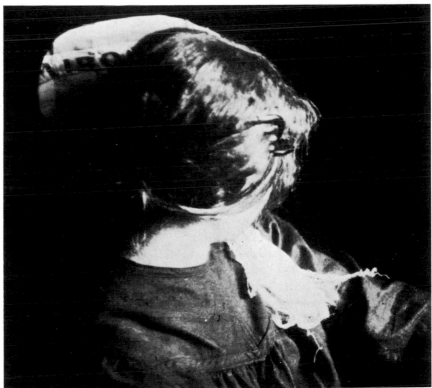

The photograph above was taken by a camera over Eva's head on 27 November 1912. It did considerable damage to her reputation.

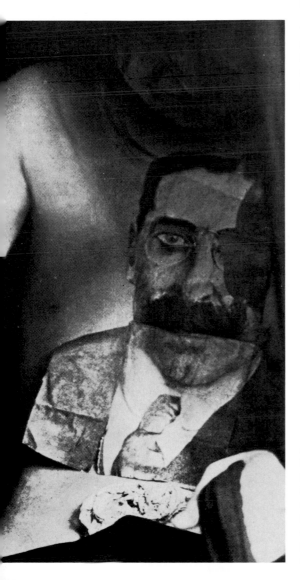

At a session on 19 January 1913, left, Eva was alone with Mme Bisson and completely nude, as she sometimes was when the two were working together. Eva nevertheless managed to produce a materialisation. However, many people found the two-dimensional image unconvincing.

itself into a perfect hand, in which nails and bones could be detected. It would then return to a blob of white and disappear.

Further testimony comes from Dr Gustave Geley's book *From the Unconscious to the Conscious:*

'From the mouth of Eva there descends to her knees a cord of white substance of the thickness of two fingers... the cord... detaches itself from the medium and moves towards me. I then see the extremity thicken like a swelling, and this terminal swelling expands into a perfectly modelled hand. I touch it... I feel the bones, and the fingers with their nails. Then the hand contracts, diminishes, and disappears in the end of the cord.'

Geley held a number of experimental sessions with Eva in 1917 and 1918 at his own laboratories. Before these seances, she was stripped, searched and dressed in a garment that was then sewn at the back and wrists. Her hands were also held in full sight outside the curtains throughout the seances.

Whatever others many have thought of Eva's strange mediumistic powers, Geley was in no doubt. 'I do not merely say: There was no trickery; I say there was no possibility of trickery... The materialisations took place under my own eyes.'

After her run of successful seances with Geley, Eva's powers seem to have declined. She visited London in 1920 and held 40 seances for the Society for Psychical Research over a two-month period. But half of these were blank and the others resulted only in weak phenomena. Although no fraud was detected, the SPR committee suggested that regurgitation could have produced the materialisations they witnessed. In 1922, Eva gave a series of 15 seances at the Sorbonne in Paris, but these were equally inconclusive. Both Eva and her materialisations then faded into obscurity.

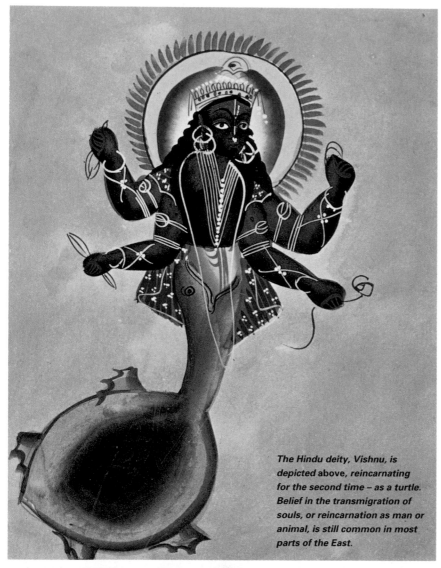

The Hindu deity, Vishnu, is depicted above, reincarnating for the second time – as a turtle. Belief in the transmigration of souls, or reincarnation as man or animal, is still common in most parts of the East.

DEATH'S GREAT ADVENTURE

SUPPOSED COMMUNICATIONS FROM BEYOND THE GRAVE SEEM TO SUGGEST THAT THE DEAD LEAD A STRENUOUS AND PURPOSEFUL EXISTENCE – IN FACT, SOME SAY THAT IN MANY WAYS THEY ARE MORE 'ALIVE' THAN WE ARE

If death is not the end of man's personality, but rather the beginning of a sort of 'pilgrim's progress', as many psychical researchers claim, what surely requires investigation is the nature of this adventure. According to one prevalent theory, the discarnate spirit, after meeting loved ones who have died before, is said to live first in a so-called 'summerland' or 'winterland', both of which are created from the individual's own habits of thought, good or bad. These are both on the ideo-plastic plane and seem to serve to break us of our earthly preoccupations and make us yearn for the benefits of higher, more spiritual faculties. But we must first undergo the judgement and the 'second death', processes that hold up a mirror to the people we were, mercilessly stripping us of any illusions about ourselves and making us realise – by momentarily becoming other people in our lives – what our actions and words had done to them.

Through experiencing the shattering but ultimately rewarding process of the 'second death', the spirit then 'earns' its entry into the second heaven. What has been shed in the trauma is only, we discover, our outer selves, or personality, which had seemed so essential previously. Personality (the word is derived from the Latin *persona,* meaning 'actor's mask') is cast away, so we now emerge as our real, 'undivided' selves.

The purpose of the second heaven is, apparently, to enable the questing spirit to grow and develop. The process takes place in what many accounts call 'the great silence'. During this period, former identity dissolves away and we experience a sense of great peace. We no longer know who or where we are, but this does not in any way prove distressing, any more than it is distressing for a butterfly to undergo the natural process of emerging from its cocoon.

At this point, the spirit loses contact with all those known during life. This is a temporary phase but said to be essential if we are to concentrate energies on coping with the new, immeasurably broader landscape we now face. There are now highly significant meetings with others – men and women with whom one feels a deep spiritual link

learn all the necessary lessons. All the opportunities will be there over the centuries for everyone. Not all of us will profit by experience or learn at the same rate, but there are many chances to put right mistakes made or opportunities lost. As Frances Banks said: 'It is still a continuation, a sequel. There is a definite continuing thread.'

This enrichment of the soul through the revelations of the past is the first step in the process of reassessment carried on in the second heaven. There are two other, equally important steps.

The first involves advice from wiser beings on how to deal with one's future earth life. The second step clarifies the true nature of the spirit's relationship with his peers, those 'old friends' with whom he has just been reunited. He now realises that they are all bound together for all eternity, united with the same overall purpose. Together, they form part of a highly important unit known as a group soul. It is said that to be with its members is to feel a deep spiritual homecoming.

The members of an earth family may be spiritually close or they may simply be genetically linked – effectively strangers on any deeper level. Their spiritual family is elsewhere. But, in the after-life, there

Most ancient cultures believed in a supernatural deity whose sole task was to preside over the dead. Part custodian and part judge, he is usually shown as a terrible figure, such as Yamantaka, Tibetan Lord of the Dead, above, or the Totonac god of ancient Mexico, Mictlantecuhtli, right.

The ninth hell, as described in Dante's Inferno and illustrated by Gustave Doré, is seen below. In this wasteland of ice and desolation, the damned soul is frozen forever, unless he confesses his sins to the superior souls who visit him.

and an intimate familiarity. This is reported as being like meeting old friends on earth with whom one has shared profound experiences. However, the spirits on this plane, although they are indeed old friends, belong to relationships formed over many lifetimes. This one fact is central to the understanding of the whole nature of the after-life. With those friends from long ago, the spirit relives ancient memories, to which his immediately previous personality had no access. Together, the members of the reunion relive past events they had shared; and as they do so, they begin to see a distinct purpose and meaning emerge from the apparently disparate and fragmentary personalities they had been in the past, for each soul has been reincarnated many times.

A CONTINUING THREAD

We now see that our lives are in no way arbitrary, but form part of a pattern and purpose that are still being worked out. Each is slowly awakening towards recognition of, and participation in, what is named his 'causal self'. This carries within it the seeds of each former life but also contains hints of what is to come in future incarnations. The second heaven is both retrospective and prospective – a plane of insight into both past and future. As the posthumous Frances Banks, a former Anglican nun, is claimed to have said: it is 'the initial stage of a journey into light, during which the surviving entity is gradually reunited with the whole soul'. We now see our past earth life in its true perspective – as a tiny fragment of a much larger prospect.

According to this theory, the past life is only the latest chapter in a long book, the 'story' of which can stretch back over many earth centuries. As the spirit begins to witness the unfolding panorama of his lives, he will inevitably realise that much in his past life was the direct consequence of actions from other, previous incarnations.

There are said to be many incarnations for most spirits, for almost everyone needs many chances to

In the statue over the Old Bailey, Britain's foremost criminal court, left, the scales and the sword carried represent two aspects of justice: mercy and retribution. According to one theory, however, absolute justice is said to be found only in the after-life – where motives are seen for what they really were in life. During the judgement, the soul suffers the pain and humiliation once inflicted on others. But kindness is also relived and rewarded.

are no such random or loose ties; the group soul comprises only members who are totally committed to their particular long-term spiritual assignment under the leadership of one who can perhaps best be likened to an elder brother. The individual members of each group are responsible to each other – and to the world – in order to fulfil the special task assigned when their group was created.

LIFE GOES ON

If such claims about conditions in the after-life – and, indeed, the purpose of life itself – are true, then our individual lives on earth can be seen in proper perspective, as part of a much greater plan. And although these accounts seem basically in harmony with the conventional Christian belief in heaven and hell, the approximately similar states exist, not as final punishments or rewards for a single earth life, but as stages in a continuing education. Each has to redeem those parts of himself that are bound by the chains of his own creation. Even in the second heaven, the processes of self-cleansing and selfless service continue. Here, the spirit learns that there are further states of bliss, but these are too intense for it yet.

Here, it becomes plain that life on earth and life between incarnations simply provide different opportunities for 'growing up'. Each spirit will pass from hard work to refreshment and on to further tasks; and although the surroundings are said to be more pleasant than on earth, basically the work is just as strenuous. It takes enormous effort for each spirit to make any lasting progress, but we are not alone and can expect the kind of help, advice and inspiration that would have been impossible on earth. Encouraged and inspired, the individual can then progress towards his own ultimate maturity.

The destiny of each soul is said to be fulfilled, only when that of the group soul is completed. This may take aeons. There are many group souls, said to range from comparatively few members to many hundreds. Frequently, a person's inner urge on earth is a reflection of the quest of his group soul, his equivalent of the Holy Grail. Everyone retains free will to depart from the group soul's set path, but the promptings of our own inner nature will, it is believed, eventually lead us back to it.

During its stay in the second heaven, the spirit learns from the 'replay' of his past lives to discover

PERSPECTIVES

THE MAN WHO WOULD BE KING

Death is said to be 'the great leveller', and nowhere is this shown more clearly than in *A Tudor Story* by the late Canon W. S. Pakenham-Walsh. This purports to tell the tale of the Canon's relationship – through several mediums – with various members of the Tudor court from the early 1920s to his death at the age of 92 in 1960. Pakenham-Walsh found that his main spiritual mission was to aid Henry VIII himself, who was angry, lost and clinging pathetically to a crown he no longer possessed, and could therefore

make no progress in the after-life. One medium had to remind 'Henry' that he was king no longer. He was furious, saying: 'I am a king. I carry royal birth and death in my hands... A king does not commit acts for which he is sorry.' The Canon enlisted the help of the 'spirits' of Anne Boleyn and Elizabeth I, among others, while also praying for the King's soul himself. For a time, Henry vacillated between apparent repentance and humility and outbursts of regal temperament. The breakthrough came when he was allowed to meet his sons – including the baby who had been stillborn, now grown up. Henry's last communication was: 'Know that Henry, once King of England, did repent'.

its true potential and what steps should be taken to fulfil it. Strengthened by the insight and love of our companions, we are now ready for a yet further expansion of consciousness, which takes place in the third heaven. This is, however, too intense an experience for many spirits to endure for very long, although it is open to us for precisely as long as we can sustain it. Although almost impossible for us to understand, communicators tell us that in the third heaven a spirit comes to the limits of its consciousness. After a brief glimpse of this plane, we find we cannot go further into it than our nature allows. Faced with such limitations, we have no choice but to return to earth.

OTHER LIVES, OTHER WORLDS

However, if our next incarnation goes well and we grow spiritually as a result, we will find that we can then proceed deeper into the third heaven. This, in turn, will enable us to make more of our succeeding earth life, for it is in the third heaven that the true nature of the group soul's task unfolds.

But what happens when a person has little more to learn from earth? Most accounts agree that a choice awaits us. We can take a leap into the great unknown, leaving this planet and its successive incarnations altogether, and begin again somewhere else. Communications are vague on this point, but they do seem to imply a new cycle of physical lives on another planet. Few, the posthumous F.W. H. Myers says, are sufficiently strong to go the first time the chance arises. Most spirits prefer to wait, helping others if needed, even if it means being reincarnated on earth yet again. A group soul will move on only when every member is ready to go. No one will be left behind.

People frequently deplore the injustices of 'life', meaning their earthly existence. But if the accounts of the after-life summarised above are substantially true, then there *is* such a thing as absolute justice; there is cause for hope, there is free will and ever-expanding consciousness. The narratives purporting to come from people in the after-life can be examined by anyone – religious beliefs and pious hopes aside – as evidence. According to certain Spiritualist beliefs, the last words of Mary, Queen of Scots – 'In my end is my beginning' – express the literal truth for everyone.

The bark painting by the Australian Aborigine artist Bunia, above, depicts aspects of the after-life.

In an early 15th-century representation, right, St Peter receives three souls at the gates of heaven. In the traditional Christian view, admission to heaven was in itself a kind of judgement, although the dreadful day of judgement was to come.

The wall painting at Tepantitla, Mexico, below, dating back more than 1,000 years, is believed to show the rain god's paradise in the after-life.

A CASE FOR REINCARNATION?

In 1956 and 1957, Emile Franckel conducted a series of live experiments for a Los Angeles television programme called *Adventures in Hypnotism*. Franckel's aim was to bring to the public's attention the possibility that individuals under hypnosis can relive previous lives. His attitude was sceptical: he believed that recollections of previous lives arose from promptings from the hypnotist or deep subconscious memory. Some of the experiences he was able to draw from his subjects, however, seemed unaccountable by this explanation. Since the hypnotist did not know his subjects, he could scarcely have induced their responses except by a series of coincidences too remarkable to be mere chance.

Yet Franckel was right to have remained sceptical. For although some of the results seemed almost miraculous, hypnosis is a mental state that many people may experience, given the right circumstances. This does not mean, however, that hypnosis is fully understood by the medical profession even today.

What appears to happen under hypnosis is that the layers of experience we have all acquired during our lives – experiences that have pushed our memory of previous existences deep into the subconscious – come to the surface. When the hypnotist suggests, for example, to a 30-year-old subject that 'It is now 1981. You are now 20 – you are waking up on your 20th birthday, tell me where you are, what is happening', the subject's life and development of the past 10 years are as if they had never been.

FANTASY PERSONALITY

But what of past lives? In many subjects there seems to be a 'shadow' – a fantasy personality that is only revealed in dreams or under hypnosis. And the suggestion is that it is this 'fantasy personality' that is revealed in regression hypnosis, not a recollection of a previous life as such.

How, then, are we to distinguish between what may be mere fantasy and a true account of a previous life? As early as 1906, the Society for Psychical Research reported the case of an unnamed clergyman's daughter who, under hypnosis, recounted her life during the reign of Richard II. In that life, she was no great lady herself – despite the claim by cynics that subjects in regression imagine themselves

The account given by Virginia Tighe, right, of her 'previous life' as 'Bridey Murphy' led Morey Bernstein, shown with her, to become a firm believer in reincarnation.

It was in 18th-century Cork, below, that Virginia Tighe claimed she had previously been born as Bridey Murphy in 1798.

to be famous people – but·an acquaintance of Maud, Countess of Salisbury, her friend Blanche Poynings, née Mowbray and Richard's mother, otherwise known as the 'Fair Maid of Kent'.

In this case, almost every historical fact stated under hypnosis was found to be true, as were details of the dress and food described by the girl. Moreover, she had no recollection of ever having read about either the period or the people.

FROM THE SUBCONSCIOUS?

Some early psychical researchers into hypnotic phenomena would wake their subjects and place their hands on a planchette board, usually screened from the subjects' view. They would then proceed to interrogate them. The planchette – it is claimed – wrote down true answers to the questions from knowledge in the subjects' subconscious minds. Under these conditions, one girl revealed that she had just read an historical romance from which every person and fact came up in her regression, except·for some minor details, though she had devised a new setting for them.

If all cases were as straightforward as this, there would be no need for further investigation, and believers in reincarnation would have to look elsewhere for evidence. How complicated the majority of cases are, however, is shown by the story of Bridey Murphy. This is no more remarkable than a hundred other cases of hypnotic regression, but was brought to the public's attention by heated debate in a number of American newspapers, as well as a film shown widely throughout the English-speaking world.

In a number of sessions taking place between November 1952 and October 1953, Morey Bernstein, an amateur American hypnotist, regressed Virginia Tighe to a life in early 19th-century Ireland. Mrs Tighe, 29 years-old at the time, a native of Maddison, Wisconsin, and resident in Chicago from the age of three until her marriage,

What appears to happen under hypnosis is that the layers of experience we have acquired during our lives – experiences that have pushed our memory of previous existences deep into the subconscious – come to the surface.

had never visited Ireland, nor had she ever had much to do with Irish people. (She strongly denied allegations to the contrary and there is evidence to support her denials.) Under hypnosis, she began to speak with an Irish accent, and said she was Bridget (Bridey) Murphy, daughter of Duncan and Kathleen Murphy, Protestants living at the Meadows, Cork. Her brother Duncan, born in 1796, married Aimée, daughter of Mrs Strayne, who was mistress of a day school attended by Bridey when she was 15.

In about 1818, she had married a Catholic, Brian MacCarthy, whose relatives she named, and they travelled by carriage to Belfast through places she

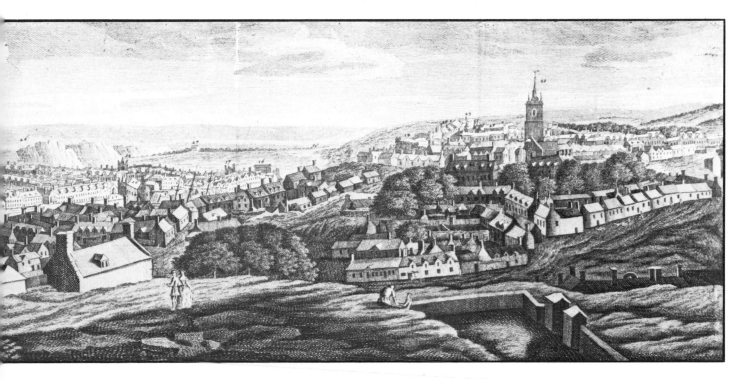

Today, what one does when kissing the Blarney Stone, right, is to lie on the back, hold on to two bars attached to the wall, lower the head and kiss the underside of the Stone. The earlier method, used at the time of 'Bridey Murphy' and shown, far right, would not have been known by Virginia Tighe, unless she had done a great deal of research.

To counter the claim that he had in some way rigged his experiments, Morey Bernstein, below, hypnotised Mrs Tighe in the presence of two witnesses.

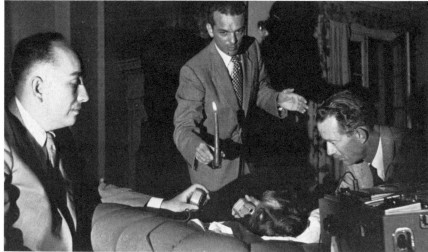

also named, but the existence of which has never been found on any map.

The couple apparently worshipped at Father John Gorman's St Theresa's Church. They shopped at stores that Bridey named, using coins correctly described for the period. In addition, Bridey produced a number of Irish words when asked, using some as they were used then, though their meaning had changed since. ('Slip', for example, referred to a child's pinafore, and not petticoat – the more common modern word.) Bridey Murphy had read some Irish mythology, knew some Irish songs and was a good dancer of Irish jigs. Indeed, at the end of one sitting, Mrs Tighe, aroused from her trance, yet not fully conscious, danced 'The Morning Jig', ending her performance with a stylised yawn. Her description of another dance was also confirmed in detail by a lady whose parents had danced it. A further telling detail was that she described the correct

procedure, as used in Bridey's day, for kissing the Blarney Stone, reputed to confer eloquence on those who manage to do so.

Bridey's story was investigated by the American magazine *Empire*, and William Barker was commissioned to spend three weeks in Ireland checking the facts 'Bridey' had given. His visit resulted in a 19,000-word report. Barker's account is typical of regression cases. Some facts were confirmed, some unconfirmed, others proved incorrect. Mysteriously, memories of insignificant detail proved true, while Bridey displayed total ignorance of more important events.

Confirmation of facts proved impossible in many instances, however. There was no way, for example, of confirming dates of birth, marriages and deaths, as no records were kept in Cork until 1864; and if the Murphy family kept records in a family bible, a customary procedure, its whereabouts are not known. No information could be discovered concerning St Theresa's Church nor Father Gorman in Belfast, but the two shops mentioned by Bridey had both existed. Bridey had also said that uillean pipes were played at her funeral, and these were found to have been customarily used because of their soft tone.

So the neutral enquirer is left puzzled. Where had Mrs Tighe learnt about uillean pipes, kissing the Blarney Stone and the names of the shops in Belfast, the existence of which was only confirmed after painstaking research? Why should her subconscious have created a vivid picture of life in Ireland at the beginning of the 19th century? And from where did she – along with many other regressed subjects with no pretence of acting ability – draw the talent to dramatise so effectively a life in another age, in another country?

Furthermore, if reincarnation is a fact, why should trivialities be remembered, while great emotional experiences that you would expect to have contributed to your development in this life be forgotten or go unmentioned?

THE OLD BELIEF
THAT A CORPSE WILL
REACT TO THE PRESENCE OF
ITS MURDERER SEEMS TO
HAVE FOUND HORRIFIC
EXPRESSION IN THE STRANGE
CASE OF A ROTTING CORPSE
THAT WINKED

Once dead and buried, few people have shown signs of life – but those who have, or are rumoured to have been reanimated, naturally enough have inspired witnesses with awe and fear. In the case of Joan Norkot, who died in 1629, her brief moment of posthumous glory did more: it was enough to point the finger of accusation – almost literally – at her murderers, and subsequently to secure their conviction.

The strange case of Joan Norkot was rediscovered in 1851, when it became one of the legal and

WITH A NOD AND A WINK

The Long Parliament of 1640, in which John Mainard, above, had sat, living long enough to see William III come to the throne in 1688, is seen top. His intellect remained as sharp as ever, and he was considered an impeccable witness to the bizarre case of Joan Norkot.

The resuscitation of Margaret Dickson, a murderer who was hanged in 1728, is depicted left. But Joan Norkot's body had begun to decompose. So how could she have revived?

SPIRITS OF THE STARS

THE VOICES OF CELEBRITIES COULD OFTEN BE HEARD AT SEANCES HELD BY MEDIUM LESLIE FLINT, FOR SHOW BUSINESS PERSONALITIES SEEMED TO FAVOUR HIM AS A CHANNEL FOR DIRECT VOICE COMMUNICATION

Leslie Flint, pictured above, was a professional medium for 42 years, during which time his seances were closely scrutinised by scientists and psychical researchers alike. Many sitters testified that the voices were indeed those of deceased persons, both famous and obscure, personally known to them. Rudolph Valentino, shown as he appeared in **The Sheik**, right, proved to be one of the most frequent communicators, though he was a silent star in life. Flint was, in turn, one of Valentino's most ardent fans.

Long after they died, Rudolph Valentino, Lionel Barrymore and Leslie Howard continued to perform before appreciative audiences – not on stage or film, of course, but in the darkened seance room of a London direct voice medium, Leslie Flint. These are but a few of the famous dead – the full list reads like a *Who's Who?* of the arts, with an additional sprinkling from other notable professions – who communicated through Flint during his 42 years as a professional medium.

It has to be said at the outset that claiming spirit contact with the famous usually arouses suspicion. Their lives, likes, and loves are usually public knowledge, and so a gifted impersonator would have no difficulty in posing as a medium and 'communicating' in a voice similar to that of any late celebrity.

But Leslie Flint's spirit visitors were not always famous. Indeed, at the height of his career, many ordinary people were able to pay a fee to sit with him; and some later testified to speaking to their relatives and friends. Flint, in such circumstances, could have known nothing about the dead who returned, and faking their voices and speech mannerisms is therefore seemingly out of the question.

Flint's spirit links with show business stars took him to the United States and to the Hollywood homes of many legendary figures; and the wealth he encountered on those visits was in stark contrast to the poverty he experienced as a child.

Flint's parents had parted when he was young, and he was brought up in a Salvation Army home. At an early age, he was credited with the ability to 'see' the dead, but this served only to separate him from other children. When he left school, he had a number of temporary jobs, including one as a grave-digger, but he was soon drawn into a Spiritualist group, and it was here that he first developed his direct voice mediumship.

It took Flint seven years to develop this rare gift, sitting twice a week. At first, he would go into into a deep trance and trumpets were used to amplify the voices of those spirits attempting to communicate with the living. As his powers grew stronger, however, he was able to remain conscious during seances and eventually dispensed with the trumpets. Sitters would assemble in the seance room,

lights would be put out, and voices would address them from thin air. Flint occasionally joined in the conversation.

Rudolph Valentino came into Flint's world at an early stage. Another medium told Flint that a man with the initials R.V. wanted to help him in a psychic way and work through him to help mankind. The spirit then appeared to the medium, dressed as an Arab. Valentino was the only person Flint thought fitted the bill – he had read a book about him as a teenager – but could not understand why the great screen lover should want to help him.

Confirmation soon came from a totally unexpected source. A letter arrived from a German woman, saying that Valentino had communicated at a seance in Munich. Valentino had apparently given Flint's name and address, and had asked the medi-

Eminent visitors from the 'other side' making guest appearances at Leslie Flint's seances included Amy Johnson, above right, who reported that there are no aeroplanes in the after-life for her to fly; George Bernard Shaw, above, who continues to write, however; as well as Leslie Howard, above left, and Lionel Barrymore, left, two giants of the screen.

um to tell Flint that he was trying to make contact. Over a period, the Munich seances also produced further items of information that corroborated statements made by Valentino to Flint through other mediums.

Sometimes Valentino spoke in his native Italian, and on one occasion he made a striking prediction. He said that Flint would visit Hollywood, stay in Valentino's Beverly Hills home and hold seances in his bedroom. Unlikely as this seemed, it all came to pass. Some years later, while visiting Hollywood, Flint was invited to visit a psychical researcher. As soon as Flint was given the address, he realised it was the former home of Rudolph Valentino. What is more, the room in which seances were held was the star's former bedroom.

Leslie Howard, Lionel Barrymore and Mrs Patrick Campbell are other stars who are said to have made an appearance at Flint's seances; and Rupert Brooke and George Bernard Shaw have returned to reveal that they are still writing. Amy Johnson, however, said she is no longer flying: it seems there are no aeroplanes in the spirit world. But they do have pianos, and Frédéric Chopin is still playing and composing, while Shakespeare continues to write plays, 400 years after his works were first performed.

Mahatma Gandi and Cosmo Gordon Lang, former Archbishop of Canterbury, also spoke at length on spiritual matters from their new vantage points in the next world; and Marylin Monroe returned to say she did not commit suicide but died from an accidental overdose of drugs. Queen Victoria sent messages to her last surviving daughter, Princess Louise, and King George V communicated to two members of his household.

Flint has described himself as the most 'tested' medium in Britain and has apparently always been willing to take part in experiments. An early investigator of his direct voice mediumship was Dr Louis Young, who had exposed several doubtful mediums in the United States. He once made Flint fill his mouth with coloured water before a seance started, in order to ensure he could not be throwing his voice. Then the lights were put out. Spirits chattered away as usual.

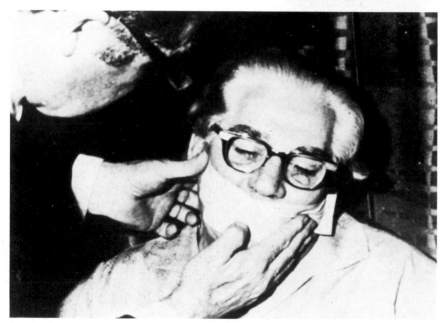

The Rev. C. Drayton Thomas, a member of the council of the Society for Psychical Research (SPR), conducted a more severe test in 1948. He placed a strip of sticking plaster across Flint's mouth and then covered it with a scarf. The medium's hands were also tied to the arms of his chair, and another cord ensured that he could not bend his head down, thus preventing him from loosening the plaster with his hands.

Once again, spirit voices spoke with their usual clarity, often very loudly. This would have been impossible if Flint were faking them. At the end of the seance, the medium was found to be bound and gagged just as he was at the start, and the clergyman had considerable difficulty in removing the sticking plaster without causing pain.

In 1972, the *Sunday Express* science correspondent, Robert Chapman, assisted by Professor William R Bennett, former head of the Department of Electrical Engineering at Columbia University, New York, and Nigel Buckmaster, an SPR member, devised an even more elaborate means of establishing the authenticity of the spirit voices. First, Flint was gagged and bound firmly to his chair. Then he

The Reverend C. Drayton Thomas, top, a member of the Society for Psychical Research, tested Flint in 1948. He was satisfied that, during the test, Flint remained bound and gagged, but the spirit voices were heard clearly throughout.

Leslie Flint's mouth was sealed with sticking plaster, as shown above, in a test conducted by the Sunday Express. To prevent any tampering with the gag, his hands were also restrained, right. The investigators heard the voices, and also saw the ectoplasmic voice box, supposedly responsible for producing them, as it materialised in thin air, just a little way from the medium's head.

was fitted with a throat microphone, designed to show whether he was producing the sounds by ventriloquism. Two television cameras were also used, together with an infra-red detector so that Flint could be observed in the dark.

Yet the voices spoke, and investigators also saw the ectoplasmic voice box, said to be used by spirit communicators, as it formed about two feet (60 centimetres) from the medium's head. 'There could be no question of these voices coming from some hidden tape recorder, furtively switched on by Flint,' Chapman concluded, 'because there was question-and-answer dialogue with the "other side".'

SPIRITS ON TAPE

Many of the voices of celebrated visitors were recorded by researchers, George Woods and Betty Greene, who kept appointments with Flint for more than 15 years, during which they compiled a library of 500 tapes. Oscar Wilde, for instance, said his new existence was quite unlike his earthly life. 'It is no longer a sin here to be human and to be natural.'

Leslie Flint retired in December 1976. The recordings made by Woods and Greene, and by many other sitters, provide a lasting reminder of his mediumship. Despite many glowing tributes, sceptics have found it easy to pick holes in some of the seance conversations. The words and mannerisms of some famous speakers are not always what we would expect.

Flint himself, after all those years of listening to spirit voices in a darkened seance room, continued to find some aspects of his own mediumship puzzling. He could not explain, for example, why some of the voices spoke only in a whisper, whereas others spoke loudly.

One other aspect of Flint's work, often overlooked in articles about him, is worth recording. Very often, sitters would sit and chat for an hour in his seance room and nothing would happen at all. Flint may have been one of the most gifted direct voice mediums of all time, but his powers could not be turned on at will.

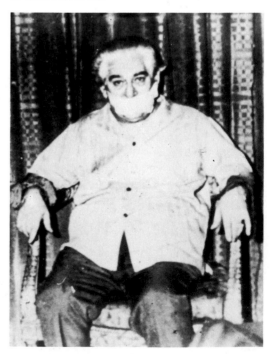

A MEDIUM UNMASKED

FOR DECADES, THE FAMOUS MEDIUM WILLIAM ROY ASTOUNDED SITTERS AT SEANCES WITH 'SPIRIT' VOICES, MATERIALISATIONS – AND INFORMATION THAT, IT WAS BELIEVED, HE COULD HAVE GAINED ONLY BY PARANORMAL MEANS

When William Roy died in August 1977, the publication *Psychic News* said of him: 'In Spiritualism's long history there has never been a greater villain. He is now in a world where he cannot cheat.' Yet there were those who would not accept that verdict, for over the years Roy had so raised false hopes among his victims that a great many of them could never face the fact that he was a fraud. And the people he duped were not always simple, ill-educated types – far from it. They included prominent society figures, among them the late W. L. Mackenzie King.

Mackenzie King's involvement began during the Second World War, when he was Prime Minister of Canada. It was a post that he had held before, but war naturally brought with it many extra responsibilities, which included top-secret visits to London to confer with the War Cabinet. It was on one of these 'hush-hush' visits that he decided to

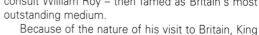

The 'medium' William Roy, above right, thrived on publicity, both good and bad. However, his early successes established his reputation among those who wanted to believe he was genuine. For example, during the Second World War, W. L. Mackenzie King, right, the Canadian Prime Minister, visited Roy under an assumed name – and was astonished to be given pertinent messages by an assortment of deceased statesmen. Yet Roy himself later confessed that this was all fraud, based on ingenious detective work that had established the identity of the sitter well in advance of the seance – enabling him to do his 'homework'.

consult William Roy – then famed as Britain's most outstanding medium.

Because of the nature of his visit to Britain, King thought it wise not to give his true name to Roy in advance of the consultation. So, on the surface, it looked as if Roy had no clue as to the real identity of his client. And yet Roy was able to give the Canadian Prime Minister a number of apparently convincing messages, and all from those who, in real life, would naturally and easily talk to a head of government. The grandest was Queen Victoria herself. Mackenzie King was thrilled as he chatted away to 'Her Majesty'.

More thrills came when Mr Gladstone 'came through' and gave a message of hope – just the kind of thing to cheer one up in the dark days of war. It was all very satisfying and comforting; so much so that the Canadian Prime Minister went back for further sessions and was overwhelmed when his dead brother and sister spoke to him.

Mackenzie King returned to Canada overjoyed and without any suspicions whatsoever about Roy – completely unaware that he had been thoroughly deceived by a scheming rogue. For Roy's 'psychic gifts' were non-existent. His sessions involved nothing more than play-acting, using fake voices and stage effects, while his 'revelations' or personal messages for the bereaved were, in fact, due to planning and trickery. So how did he do it?

His tricks were usually based on techniques that had been used at the height of the Spiritualist craze in the 19th century. He had added a few of his own but, in the main, he kept to stunts that had been well-tried by other tricksters before him. In fact, Roy had found most of his tricks carefully explained in a book called *Behind the Scenes with the Mediums*. This enlightening book was written by David Abbott in 1907 and published in the USA, although a few copies were sold in England by the Magical and Unique Novelty Company of London. Roy had the good fortune to find one of these copies and it set his mind reeling. In the pages of this obscure book was all the advice that Roy need-ed in order to set up a lucrative business. From then on, as far as he was concerned, Abbott's book was worth its weight in gold.

The equipment used by Roy and his accomplice in their bogus seances is shown below. The accomplice collected as much information as he could about the sitters and conveyed this to Roy from the next room by means of a cordless telephone. The connection was made by Roy placing his copper-soled shoes on metal tacks hidden in the carpet, which were wired to cables running through the wall. Wires that ran up Roy's trouser-leg, below right, ended in a miniature hearing aid – through which he could hear his accomplice, but the sitters could not.

" BUT ROY WAS FAMOUS FOR MORE THAN THE MESSAGES HE GAVE – IT WAS THE DRAMA WITH WHICH HE DELIVERED THEM THAT BROUGHT HIM RENOWN... SOMETIMES THERE WOULD EVEN BE TWO VOICES SPEAKING SIMULTANEOUSLY. "

By the time Roy set himself up as a medium, he had mastered most of the tricks in the book. He even worked out a few refinements. His clients innocently walked into a trap every time they visited his home: they were expected to leave all coats and bags in a special cloakroom, and this gave Roy's accomplice a chance to search through their belongings for bits of useful information. Moreover, clients were kept waiting before each seance began. And as they chatted to pass the time away, hidden microphones picked up their words. By these means, Roy always knew more about his clients than they dreamed possible. Sometimes he would even overhear them name the dead relatives they hoped to contact. In this way, every sitting was neatly rigged beforehand. And when Roy ran out of authentic titbits, he was adroit enough to bluff his way out of trouble – which was partly done by calling on colourful 'spirit guides'. There was one called Joey, another called Dr Wilson and, best of the lot, a Red Indian called Tinka. Tinka was not only fashionable – Red Indians being 'in' as spirit guides – he was invaluable; for, if the questions became awkward, he would just sulk and grunt: 'No can answer... Me just simple Indian' – which would quickly smooth over any trickier parts of the evening.

The microphones and searches of coats and bags were not, however, the only preparations. Once Roy knew the names of his clients, he checked on their families at the registry in Somerset House, or looked up death notices and entries in *Who's Who*. He even contacted other fake mediums for extra information.

But his most masterly research involved his initial session with Mackenzie King. In that case, he had no opportunity to go through the Prime Minister's pockets and no chance to listen in to his conversation. All he knew in advance was that he was to have a sitting with a 'distinguished person'. And all he knew about the booking was that it was

Although the Spiritualist world knew of Roy's fraud as early as 1952, it was not until 1958 that the story made banner headlines in the Sunday Pictorial, above left. Curiously, Roy seemed almost to delight in confessing, as well as in explaining how he accomplished his bogus effects. He revealed, among other tricks, how he used to make his 'spirit trumpet' fly around the darkened seance room: quite simply, it was attached to the end of a telescopic rod, which could be hidden in the hand, as above, or extended, top.

made by a member of the Duke of Connaught's staff. That was little enough to go on, but Roy had to start somewhere – so he studied everything he could find about the Duke of Connaught. And he discovered that the Duke had been Governor General of Canada from 1911 to 1916. As soon as he read that, Roy made a brilliant deduction – this mysterious visitor could easily be a distinguished Canadian friend of the Duke. And the most distinguished Canadian known to embrace Spiritualism was their Prime Minister – Mackenzie King.

FAKE VOICES

Roy was so convinced that his deduction was right that he began practising passages in the voices of Gladstone and Queen Victoria, specifically tailored to King's character. The Queen's high-pitched voice was something of a strain; but by the time Mackenzie King turned up, it was good enough to fool him and make him want to know more about the communications.

But Roy was famous for more than the messages he gave – it was the drama with which he delivered them that brought him renown. He could make a luminous trumpet float throught the air in the darkened seance room and induce 'spirit voices' to speak through it. Sometimes there would even be two voices speaking simultaneously. And, remarkably enough, he could even produce extra voices in full light.

When he appeared at public meetings, he worked even more baffling stunts. In 1947, at Kingsway Hall, London, for instance, his hands were tied to the arms of a chair; his mouth was filled with coloured water and his lips were sealed with sticking plaster – yet he still produced 'spirit' voices. After the plaster was removed, his mouth was found to be still full of the coloured water – so fakery seemed ruled out. But Roy was responsible for all the voices, even when his mouth was filled

The system worked beautifully, especially as the earphone could double as a miniature loudspeaker. But it had its limits, so a second connection to the other room was called for. This was provided by a dummy power socket on the wall, which was wired not to the mains but to an amplifier. Thus, Roy was able to plug a cable into it and energize a miniature loudspeaker fixed on the tip of his telescopic rod. While his assistant's voice came through this speaker, Roy imitated one of his 'guides' and threw in occasional comments in his own voice. Small wonder that he was famed for his spellbinding sessions.

Roy's trickery was first exposed in 1952 when he fell out with his assistant – who promptly paid a visit to the offices of *Psychic News*. There, he opened a large suitcase and took out the apparatus used to fake the seances. It was all there, from telescopic rod to shoes fitted with copper plates. It looked like the end for Roy.

But there proved to be a problem, for the assistant did not want the matter to go any further. Following this, Roy promised to give up mediumship and leave the country, saying that he wanted to make a new start in South Africa. In fact, he did leave England and the whole sorry affair was silently laid to rest – or so it seemed.

SUPREME TRICKSTER

However, old habits die hard; and within a few years, Roy was organizing seances in South Africa. But then he had the supreme cheek to return to Britain and even started up his seances again. However, he had gone too far; this proved too much for the rest of the Spiritualist fraternity and one of their papers, *Two Worlds*, finally exposed him as a fraudulent medium.

Dramatic scenes followed this newspaper report. Roy's wife attacked the paper's editor with a riding crop, and Roy himself started a lawsuit against the editor. Roy's wife was fined £3 for the assault and Roy could afford to pay the fine with a smile – for he knew that, in effect, his lawsuit meant that he could go on milking his clients because his action had discouraged any further newspaper comment on the case until after the court hearing. Court actions, he knew, sometimes take years before they are heard – which is precisely what happened in Roy's case.

Roy carried on his fakery until February 1958. Then he dropped the lawsuit he knew he could never win and he agreed to pay costs to the editor of *Two Worlds*. Following that, he brazenly sold his story to the *Sunday Pictorial*. It was published in five instalments, and readers marvelled at how he had cheated his way to fame and fortune. At the end of the series, Roy wrote: 'I know that, even after this confession, I could fill the seance rooms again with people who find it a comfort to believe I am genuine.'

At the time that sounded like hot air or bravado, but Roy went on to make his boast come true. He set up shop under the name Bill Silver, and for years ran his old racket without challenge. Astonishingly, he numbered among his clients many who knew his real identity and who were fully aware of his history of cold-blooded fraud, cynical confessions and publicity-seeking.

and sealed. For him, that was just a minor inconvenience. In the darkness, it was easy for him to bend his head down and loosen the plaster with one tied hand – then the water was ejected through a rubber tube into a small container in his breast pocket. At the end of the evening, the water was sucked back up again, the plaster was smoothed back into place, and everyone was duly overawed at this astonishing display of Roy's psychic powers.

The private seances were a different matter. Most of the voices were produced by Roy but some were provided by his assistant, while others were tape-recordings. In that way, Roy was able to produce more than one voice at a time. And the methods he used – apart from the tape-recordings – were all drawn from that invaluable book by Abbott.

First, the trumpet flew through the air on the end of a telescopic rod – just as Abbott described. And the assistant in the next room passed information through to Roy by a telephone – again, exactly as in the book. Of course, the telephone connection was made without cords, for that would have given the game away. Instead, Roy wore copper plates on the soles of his shoes and these were soldered to thin wires that ran up the legs of his trousers and through his jacket to a small earphone on his wrist. To link up with his assistant, he had only to put his feet on to metal carpet tacks and he was connected – for the tacks were wired up to cables running through the wall.

Roy shows, above, how to evade test conditions at a 'direct voice' seance, while one of his 'spirits' proves not to be so convincing when seen in a good light, below.

CREATIONS OF THE SUBCONSCIOUS?

UNDER HYPNOSIS, A PERSON CAN ASSUME AN ENTIRELY DIFFERENT PERSONALITY. BUT IS THIS AN ECHO OF A PAST LIFE OR A CREATION OF THE SUBCONSCIOUS MIND? HERE WE SUM UP THE EVIDENCE THAT HYPNOSIS OFFERS FOR – AND AGAINST – REINCARNATION

F ew accounts of 'previous lives' recalled by people under hypnosis are free of inconsistencies or historical inaccuracies. But these in themselves are not sufficient to destroy the possibility that some cases of hypnotic regression are true reports of events that happened in a previous life. Psychologists have developed their own theories to account for hypnotic regression. And some, while denying that reincarnation is involved, accept that something outside the range of normal scientific explanation is at work. Broadly, then, there are two views taken of hypnotic regression: the 'normal' and the 'paranormal'.

According to the 'normal' view, suggestibility plays a large part in the relationship between the hypnotist and his subject. Indeed, the knowledge that the hypnotist is conducting an experiment in regression may be enough for the subject to respond by providing details of an imagined past life that are manufactured for the purpose. There is certainly evidence that the subconscious creative capacity of human beings is extraordinarily powerful. Under hypnosis, the subject may display a talent for acting, drawing, painting, writing or musical performance or composition far exceeding not only his own conscious ability but also the ability of most other people. The manufacture of a past life simply to gratify the hypnotist's expectations may therefore be carried out and enacted at short notice and with startling conviction.

The material for such 'lives' may come from many sources. A dream that is felt to be significant because of its vividness or recurrence, for instance, can sometimes provide the foundation. Alternatively, there may have been subconscious imprinting by parents or others in the subject's childhood – or even earlier, for there is evidence that the foetus can hear and register impressions in the womb during the months immediately prior to birth.

There are other possibilities, too. An individual who is widely read in historical material could use such knowledge to create a number of different lives, each focused on a different period of history. Ideas that are communicated, either consciously or subconsciously, by the hypnotist can also be picked up and elaborated upon by the hypnotic subject, while even someone unversed in hypnosis can elicit a response from the subject by innocently asking leading questions.

Hypermnesia, arousal of acutely detailed memories, and cryptomnesia, the tapping of hidden memories, may also provide reincarnation material; and events recalled in this way may be stage-managed by the subconscious to create a fantasy past life based on experiences in this incarnation. There are instances of hypermnesia, for example, in which a

The automatic painting, above, was created by London housewife Madge Gill, who died in 1961. She ascribed such drawing to the intervention of a spirit called 'Myrninerest' – but could it have been the work of her subconscious mind?

The 17th-century so-called little Prophets of Cévennes, right, are said to have been able to preach even before they could converse. Was genetic memory perhaps at work?

reader in a library glances at a printed page of, say, some archaic language for a few minutes and, decades later, is able to reproduce the same text in the minutest detail.

Such stage-management by the subconscious mind may provide an explanation for the case of Virginia Tighe, an American, who was regressed under hypnosis to become 'Bridey Murphy', who had apparently lived around 100 years previously. The *Chicago American,* in its exposé of the case, argued that certain facts disproved the theory of reincarnation.

As a child, Mrs Tighe had lived in Chicago, opposite an Irish family by the name of Corkell, and one of her childhood friends had been Kevin Corkell. 'Bridey Murphy' said she had lived in Cork and had a friend called Kevin. Even more revealing, the newspaper claimed, was the fact that Mrs Corkell's maiden name was Bridey Murphy; and Mrs Tighe's sister had fallen down a flight of stairs in circumstances strangely similar to the fall that caused Bridey's death, as revealed under hypnosis.

But this evidence does not succeed in either disproving or establishing the argument that 'Bridey Murphy' was just the childhood memory of Mrs Tighe or that Virginia Tighe was the reincarnation of 'Bridey Murphy'. Thus, the case remains open.

In Focus

CAYCE'S COSMIC KNOWLEDGE

The famous American clairvoyant Edgar Cayce was an active churchgoer all his life, and was inclined to dismiss reincarnation as un-Christian. One day, however, in 1923, a small boy climbed upon his lap and said: 'We were hungry together at the river.' This shook Cayce. He once had a dream, known only to his immediate family, of fleeing from Indians on the Ohio River and being killed. An old friend and religious thinker, Arthur Lammers, then persuaded Cayce to use the trance state to investigate a possible past life.

At first, Cayce was wary of such an unorthodox idea. But after examining the results – he appeared to have been a high priest in ancient Egypt, an apothecary in the Trojan War and a British soldier during the colonisation of America – he began to believe.

Cayce said that the readings of past lives that he went on to provide were culled from a universal or 'Akashic record' (from the Sanskrit *akasha,* meaning the fundamental etheric substance of the Universe). These are complete records of everything done and said since the beginning of time.

The recall of genetic, racial and folk memories provides another possible explanation for regression phenomena. We undoubtedly inherit some traits from our ancestors, but whether we inherit their memories is another matter. The claim that genetic memory can account for such cases as the Little Prophets of Cévennes – French Huguenot children who, in times of persecution in the 17th century, preached Protestant sermons with ecstatic fervour before they could hardly talk – is usually countered by the argument that, even if you accept the considerable contemporary evidence, there are still too few cases to justify the theory.

It is also said that some former lives described by subjects under hypnosis are too close to the present for such memory to have taken effect.

FOLK FEARS

According to this way of thinking, the last of Jane Evans' six recorded lives, that of Sister Grace, for instance, was not only too close to her in time, but she was also a celibate nun, so there could be no physical bridge across which her memories could have been passed to Jane. But there may be, in all of us, archetypal 'folk fears' – of being burnt as a witch or heretic, for example, or of suffering from chronic poverty – which, under hypnosis, are expressed as events in a 'previous life'. A Jewish girl, too young to have known of concentration camps except as a fact of history, nevertheless dreamed vividly and recurrently as a child that she was immured in one.

officer in the Irish Guards, born in 1850, who had a number of French mistresses and was killed in 1892 by a fall fom his horse. This character seems closely modelled on a certain Timothy O'Malley who, in real life, ran the subject's grandfather out of Ireland and was later killed in an accident with his horse.

Acknowledging the historical inaccuracy – the Irish Guards were not formed until 1900 – E.S. Zolic, who investigated the case, ascribes the former 'life' to the subject's identification with his grandfather's enemy, the real O'Malley.

Another subject became 'Dick Wonchalk' (1850-1876), who seems to have led a solitary life after his family was massacred by Indians when he was a child. But this 'life' could be taken as a reflection of the subject's real feelings of isolation in childhood, his concern about loneliness, fear of not being accepted by people, and self-blame for his inadequacies.

There may indeed be a definite purpose behind the incubation of such lives. The physical body, when attacked by disease, produces antibodies that counterattack the invaders and, in a strong body, eventually gain supremacy. It is conceivable that,

Images of a Nazi concentration camp, such as the one shown left, recurred in the vivid dreams of a Jewish girl who was too young to have known about them.

The illustration below depicts a witch being burnt at the stake in France in 1680. Deaths like this are frequently described under regression hypnosis, but may be a reflection of a commonly held fear of a violent end.

Alexander Cannon, bottom, was a Spiritualist whose hypnotic subjects also used Spiritualist vocabulary to describe intermission periods between their former lives. Were they perhaps influenced telepathically by his own beliefs?

Dissociated personality – in which the human body may be inhabited by up to a dozen or more 'individuals' – is a rare form of mental illness. But sometimes, when apparently normal people are hypnotised for therapeutic purposes, such a personality, or personalities, may emerge whose existence would otherwise never have been suspected.

HIDDEN PERSONALITIES

It may be that some people harbour compensatory personalities in their subconscious, either as a means of expressing a personality whose fulfilment has been denied them by circumstances or as a way of making up for some quality missing in their conscious lives. An argument often presented against this possibility, however, is that the majority of regressed lives are dull or unhappy, and most end in violent death.

Indeed, the same argument may be raised against the psychological explanation of subconscious role-playing. When we daydream consciously, we see ourselves as happier, more fulfilled people than we really are. Why should so much subliminal role-playing, then, emphasize the dull, the sordid and the wretched?

Students of psychodynamics – the examination of personality in terms of past and present experiences with regard to motivation – believe that regressed lives are based on unconscious memory, revealing a connection between the subject's conscious personality and the one that emerges in the course of hypnosis.

In one particular case, for example, it was found that the subject's relationship with his grandfather lay at the heart of his regressive 'imaginings'. The grandfather disliked his grandson – the subject – because he had once borrowed his grandfather's mare without permission. This had aroused the old man's fury, and he told the parents that their son had bad blood in him – something which the grandson overheard. Under hypnosis, the subject became 'Brian O'Malley', claiming to be a British

" FROM THE VERY BEGINNING, VASSY AND I BOTH BELIEVED WE HAD KNOWN EACH OHER IN AT LEAST ONE PREVIOUS LIFETIME. FOR THAT REASON AS WELL AS MANY OTHERS, WE WERE SPIRITUALLY COMPATIBLE. *"*

**SHIRLEY MACLAINE,
DANCING IN THE LIGHT**

The actor Fredric March is seen, below and below right, in two very different guises in the 1931 film version of Dr Jekyll and Mr Hyde. The characters of Jekyll, and his alter ego Mr Hyde, symbolise conscious and subconscious forces inside all people that can come to the surface under hypnosis.

One hypnotised subject told how, in another life, he had become an orphan after his family had died at the hands of Indians attacking their wagon train – a scene depicted above. Psychologists think this 'life' dramatised his deep sense of loneliness and social inadequacy.

in similar fashion, the mind produces mental anti-bodies, which by 'explaining' present weakness in terms of a past life, heal the patient psychologically and psychically. Thus, the American high-board diver, who was unaccountably panic-stricken by a shadow in the water as she was about to dive and could not jump, may have neutralized her irrational fear under hypnosis by 'explaining' it as the result of an event in a former life, in which – just as she was about to jump in the water – she saw the shadow of an alligator that then killed her. This 'explanation' in turn removed the fear, which no longer appeared irrational.

Paranormal explanations for past life accounts include telepathic tapping of the hypnotist's mind and also clairvoyance – the obtaining of information from, for example, closed books in libraries that the subject has never visited. There is even a theory of General-ESP or Super-ESP, which suggests that the mind of the hypnotised subject can have access to

information in books or in other people's minds. By selecting and arranging this from many sources, the subject may present an accurate account of an actual life once lived.

Spiritualists, meanwhile, who reject reincarnation, ascribe the accuracies reported in regressed lives to efficient spirit communication, and inaccuracies to communication difficulties. It is just as hard, they say, for spirits to communicate with us as for us to break through to them. Some people, however, claim that it is from the Akashic records of everything said and done since the world began that the details in regressed lives are obtained, although why particular lives should be selected and why the subject usually fails to show any other psychic ability are not explained.

So it is that the nature of past life regression remains elusive. In time, perhaps, we may come to understand whether it is indeed a matter of memory or merely invention.

SURGEON FROM THE OTHER SIDE

IT WAS A PERSONAL TRAGEDY THAT TRIGGERED ISA NORTHAGE'S EXTRAORDINARY PSYCHIC ABILITIES. IT ALL STARTED WITH CLAIRVOYANCE AND WAS TO CLIMAX WITH MATERIALISATIONS OF A DECEASED SURGEON WHO PERFORMED OPERATIONS ON THE LIVING

In 1916, a young woman named Isa Phillips was eagerly planning her wedding day when, in a vivid and horrifying vision, she saw her husband-to-be, Kit – at the time, away on active service – shot and fall from his horse: a few days later, she received news of his death.

A friend brought Kit's personal belongings home to Isa, and described to her how Kit had died: it confirmed Isa's psychic vision in every detail. Isa had also seen this man, Jack Northage, in her vision – he had gone to Kit's assistance – and, as things turned out, he also had a large part to play in Isa's

When a spirit guide advised medium Isa Northage, above, to concentrate on healing, she started a sanctuary at Pinewoods, in the beautiful grounds of Newstead Abbey, Nottinghamshire, below.

future. They became firm friends, and were eventually married in 1919.

Not long after this first demonstration of her psychic abilities, Isa began to hear a man's voice, which guided her whenever she was in danger. She also began to develop clairvoyant powers.

After the war, Isa formed a small orchestra, which flourished for a time. Then she began 'seeing' faces and people in front of her music stand while she was playing. These 'spirits' indicated that they wanted to speak to her and give her tunes that had a special meaning for their loved ones.

Almost everyone in the Western world is afraid of dying. The fear is so widespread and has such profound effects that the medical profession has coined a word for it: thanatophobia (*Thanatos* is the Greek for 'death').

The fear itself is natural enough – but what exactly are we afraid of? The answer differs greatly from one person to another. One fears the pain and the indignities that terminal illness may bring; another fears divine judgement; someone else, on the contrary, is afraid that there is nothing after death but oblivion; and another is anxious not for himself but for dependents left behind. But to most people, death is simply 'the unknown', too fearful to be contemplated. The result is a taboo on any discussion of the topic.

This conspiracy of silence inevitably adds to the burdens of those who are approaching their death. Today, in developed countries, most terminally-ill patients are sent to hospital – removed from home to endure painful and frequently embarrassing treatment, and finally dying among strangers. They are facing the greatest trauma of their lives, yet all too often no one will even talk with them about their imminent death. Visitors try to maintain the fiction that all will be well; discussing the making of a will is often considered to be in dubious taste; and even if surrounded by people, the dying patient is appallingly isolated.

But a new profession has been created to meet such needs – that of counselling for the dying. One of the most remarkable workers in this field is Dr Elisabeth Kübler-Ross, an American who has been counselling the dying, from tiny children to old people, since the 1960s. But what is probably the most important result of her work is sometimes a source of embarrassment to fellow professionals. In 1974, Dr Kübler-Ross made this uncompromising statement: 'Before I started working with dying patients, I did not believe in life after death. I now believe in it beyond all shadow of a doubt.'

Extraordinary personal experiences have convinced her of this. But before they occurred, what she had seen of the deaths of others sometimes also suggested that they marked the transition to a new life.

COSMIC CONSCIOUSNESS

TERMINALLY ILL PATIENTS HAVE GAINED REASSURANCE FROM A REMARKABLE DOCTOR WHO BELIEVES SHE HAS EXPERIENCED THE PROCESS OF DYING AND THEREFORE NOW HAS NO FEAR OF DEATH

Figures of angels and the symbol of the cross, found in profusion in every Christian graveyard as above, express a profound hope for a life beyond the grave – a hope that goes hand in hand with a deep fear of death. Yet some who have been on the very brink of dying claim to know that there is an afterlife.

Dr Kübler-Ross has observed that there are five stages that a terminally ill person can go through – though he or she may not reach the last stage before death comes. The first is denial, accompanied by avoidance of others: 'It can't happen to me – and I won't talk to anyone.' This is followed by anger: 'Why me? Why not someone older, less well-educated, less useful?' The third stage is bargaining: 'If I do as I'm told, you will make me better won't you?' Then comes depression: 'I really am dying – me, dying!' Finally, comes acceptance.

It is at this last stage that nurses often report the patient's behaviour changing drastically. He may

hear voices or see visions of dead friends and relatives who, seemingly, have come to escort him into a new existence. (Such hallucinations have been dubbed 'take-away visions' by thanatologist Dr Raymond Moody.) The patient may also speak of recurring images of tunnels, lights, and feelings of peace, like those occurring during out-of-the-body experiences.

THE HAPPINESS BEYOND

In her work, Dr Kübler-Ross has encountered many such cases. She has also spoken with many patients who had clinically 'died' but who were subsequently resuscitated. Their stories of leaving the body and experiencing great happiness, even excitement, are remarkably consistent. Few wanted to 'come back', and usually only out of a sense of responsibility for a loved one who was left behind. Most significantly, almost everyone who had experienced a short period of 'death' had no fear of dying finally. As one doctor who resuscitated a woman patient remarked: 'I have worked with people many times to get them to accept their death; but this was the first time I have ever had to get someone to accept *life*.'

Of course, not everyone dies peacefully, without pain or distress. In many people, the will to live is very strong and results in a battle, as in the case of Wallace Abel. In 1975, he found himself in the Scottsdale Memorial Hospital in Arizona, USA, suffering from a heart attack. During his stay, his heart stopped twice, and both times he was resuscitated. Recalling the second occasion, he said:

'Suddenly there was a tugging at my midsection. A transparent figure of me was struggling to leave my body. I recognised it immediately, but my body seemed to refuse to let [it] go... My image struggled, twisted, pulled. Suddenly, I realised I was witnessing my own struggle for life.'

A soul joyfully and trustingly leaves its body escorted by angels, in William Blake's picture, below. People near death often see beings – usually deceased loved ones – who have apparently come to act as guides into the next stage of existence.

Not all thanatologists believe that these 'near death' experiences are valid evidence of some kind of life beyond the death of the body. Another American, Dr Russell Noyes, a psychiatrist at the University of Iowa Medical School, studied the stories of 114 resuscitated patients – which included accounts of out-of-the-body experiences, floating sensations, freedom from pain and a sense of joy. He concluded that such experiences merely represent 'depersonalisation', an 'emergency mechanism, or sort of reflex action, which is genetically programmed to help us over the greatest trauma of our lives, that of death. Noyes does not believe that any of the tales of the dying are anything more than hallucinations.

RELIVING DEATH

The strength of Kübler-Ross' conviction, however, rests – as we have said – on her own amazing personal experiences. In the early 1970s, after a tiring day in which she had counselled several dying patients, Dr Kübler-Ross lay down to rest. Suddenly, she had the experience of leaving her body. She learned later that someone checked her pulse and respiration at this time and thought she was dead.

When Kübler-Ross 'returned' to her body, she felt that she had discovered that consciousness can leave the body under certain circumstances in life – and presumably does so at death, permanently. What is more, she felt that she now knew what it was like to die. But an even stranger and far more traumatic experience was to follow, transforming her whole outlook on life – and especially death. One night, she was finding it difficult to sleep when suddenly:

'I had one of the most incredible experiences of my life... I went through every single death of every single one of my thousand patients. And I mean the physical pain, the... agony, the screaming for help. The pain was beyond description. There was no

time to think and no time for anything except that, twice, I caught a breath, like between two labour pains. I was able to catch my breath for a split second and I pleaded – I guess with God – for a shoulder to lean on, for one human shoulder, and I visualized a man's shoulder that I could put my head on.

'And a thunderous voice came: "You shall not be given". Those words. And then I went back to my agony and doubling up in bed. But I was awake, it wasn't a dream. I was reliving every single death of every one of my dying patients.'

Again the voice thundered: 'You shall not be given'. Gasping for breath, she raged at it: 'I have helped so many and now no one will help me.' But at that moment, the realisation came to her that she must do it alone, that no one can do it for her. And in place of the unimaginable suffering came 'the most incredible rebirth experience'. She described it as follows:

'Everywhere I looked in the room – my legs, the closet, the window – everything started to vibrate into a million molecules. Everything vibrated at this incredible speed... Behind was a sunrise, the brightest light you can imagine... the light was full and open, like the whole sun was there... the vibrations stopped, and the million molecules, including me... fell into one piece... and I was part of that one. And I finally thought: "I'm okay, because I'm part of all this".'

She began to see every pebble, leaf and bird – everything that is – as being part of a whole 'alive universe', seemingly experiencing what the mystics have termed 'cosmic consciousness'. In some way, too, the experience gave her insight into the continuity of all things, including the spirit before and after death.

However, this dreadful, yet enlightening, experience was not to be the final paranormal event in her life. Some time later, as she sat in her office in

The souls of the dying in a 19th-century New York hospital are depicted, left, as seen by the clairvoyant Andrew Jackson Davis, the 'seer of Poughkeepsie'. Davis claimed to be able to see into the world of spirits, which he called 'Summerland'. But departure from life could be blighted by the grim conditions of the hospitals of the time. Problems exist today, too, since even a patient surrounded by medical staff, as below, may be intolerably lonely.

a hospital in Chicago, a former patient of hers walked in to thank her personally for all she had done and to encourage her to continue in her good work. Kübler-Ross recognised Mrs Schwartz instantly, and thought she must be hallucinating. Mrs Schwartz was dead. Then the doctor's scientific training asserted itself: she presented the apparition with a pen and paper and asked her to write a note, dated and signed. Mrs Schwartz duly did so and went away. The handwriting has since been compared by experts with that of the dead woman and vouched for as hers.

VOICE FROM BEYOND

On a further occasion, Kübler-Ross tape-recorded the voice of another deceased patient, Willie. As she put it:

'I understand that this is very far out, and I don't want people to be less sceptical. I am sceptical myself. The scientist in me needed Mrs Schwartz to sign a paper, though I knew she was in my office. And I needed a tape recording of Willie's voice. I still listen to it and think it's one big, incredible dream. I am still filled with this incredible sense of awe and miracle.'

An acknowledged pioneer in the growing field of thanatology, Dr Kübler-Ross has written a major work, *On Death and Dying*. It is, in many respects, essential reading for doctors, nurses, social workers and others who are continually faced with the problems of coping with terminally ill patients. Yet her certainty about the afterlife, her out-of-the-body experiences and her descriptions of cosmic consciousness have proved a shocking embarrassment to many members of the medical profession. Her work is freely quoted, and her vast practical experience drawn on, but very few students care to discuss her spiritual discoveries. The dying patient who is lucky enough to be counselled by Dr Kübler-Ross may well never hear her speak of an afterlife unless she is specifically asked to do so. But to her five stages in the process of dying, she has now, privately, added a sixth: the afterlife.

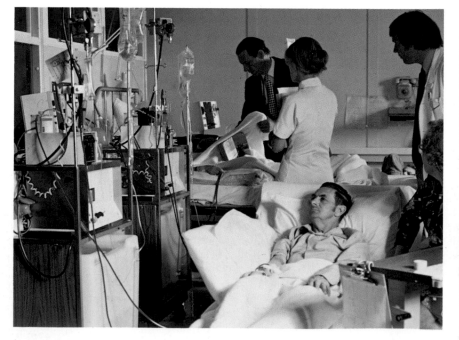